Happy Entertaining!

Marlene Sorosky

Marlene Sorosky's
Cookery for Entertaining

Entertaining With Ease 2
Freeze Now—Enjoy Later 4
Gala Garnishes 6
Festive Fare 15
Brunch Get-Togethers 31
Luncheons 49
Buffet Suppers 74
Dinner Parties 93
Cocktail Parties 110
Dessert Buffets 129
Beverages 148
How Much For How Many 157
Metric Chart 158
Index 158

ANOTHER BEST-SELLING COOKERY VOLUME FROM H.P. BOOKS

Co-Author: Linda Kreisberg; Publisher: Helen Fisher; Editor: Carlene Tejada; Senior Editor: Jon Latimer; Editor-in-Chief: Carl Shipman; Art Director: Don Burton; Book Design: Kathy Marie; Typography: Connie Brown, Cindy Coatsworth; Food Stylists: Marlene Sorosky, Linda Kreisberg, Janet Pittman; Photography: George de Gennaro Studios.

The author wishes to thank Gisela Weidt, Julia Child, Rosemary Manell, Jacques Pépin and Madame Liane Kuony for generously sharing their experience and wisdom, and especially her many students whose enthusiastic response encouraged her to write this book.

Published by H.P. Books, P.O. Box 5367, Tucson, AZ 85703   602/888-2150
ISBN: Softcover, 0-89586-019-8; Hardcover, 0-89586-020-1
Library of Congress Catalog Card Number, 78-71788 © 1979 Fisher Publishing, Inc.
Printed in U.S.A.

Cover Photo: Watermelon Whale, pages 10 and 11.

Entertaining With Ease

Wouldn't you like to give a party that has a fabulous centerpiece? Wouldn't it be miraculous if the food looked perfect, tasted superb and the beverage and dessert were exquisite? And how about a party with enough food to go around, but not so much that you'll be eating the leftovers for weeks to come?

This book can make it happen. Begin by deciding what kind of a party you want. Let the occasion reflect your mood. If autumn makes you exuberant and full of warmth toward your friends, consider the Bowl Game Buffet, page 86. If the breezes are balmy and you're just a bit lazy, plan the Summer Night Barbecue, page 100. If you don't feel up to a big dinner or a late evening, why not have a Festive Brunch? The menu is on page 37.

Entertaining today is more casual and less work than it was in the past. The emphasis is on comfort for your guests and convenience for yourself. If you don't want to bother with a tablecloth, by all means use place mats. Experiment with the things you like and don't be afraid to be different. Originality in casual entertaining is refreshing!

SERVING YOUR GUESTS

There are several ways you can serve your guests. Choose the one that is most convenient for you.

From a Buffet—The guests line up at a table or several tables to choose their own food. When they have filled their plates, they sit down at another table or places in the room you have designated. Be sure each guest has a place to sit and a place to rest a glass or plate. Silver and napkins are usually on the buffet table, but they may also be in the area where the guests will be sitting, just so they are handy.

Make Ahead Makes It Easy

Once you have decided on a menu, go over each recipe and write down the steps of preparation and when each step should be done. At least two days before making a recipe, assemble the ingredients.

This includes chopping and slicing ingredients that require it and refrigerating them in airtight containers. Here is a checklist to use as a guide in making your preparation schedule.

1 MONTH AHEAD
☐ Make out guest list and send out invitations.

ANYTIME THE MONTH BEFORE THE PARTY
Make and freeze:
☐ Appetizers   ☐ Sauces
☐ Breads   ☐ Desserts
☐ Make and freeze whatever portion of a recipe may be made in advance.

3 DAYS AHEAD
☐ Chop and measure foods, such as nuts or chopped vegetables for sauces or casseroles, that may be refrigerated in plastic bags .

2 DAYS AHEAD
Prepare foods that may be refrigerated and store covered in serving dishes, if possible.
☐ Molded salads   ☐ Sauces
☐ Salad dressings   ☐ Desserts
☐ Chop and slice salad ingredients; refrigerate in plastic bags.

1 DAY AHEAD
☐ Remove frozen foods that require overnight to thaw from freezer and thaw as directed.

☐ Prepare casseroles, vegetables, desserts or any dishes that may be refrigerated overnight.
☐ Wash salad greens, wrap in paper towels and put in plastic bags; refrigerate.
☐ Prepare fruit for salad or desserts. Cover with plastic wrap and refrigerate.
☐ Place platters and all serving forks and spoons on the table. Tag each platter with the name of the food it will hold so you won't forget to serve a dish which may be in the oven or refrigerator.

DAY OF THE PARTY
☐ Remove all food that has not been thawed from the freezer and thaw as directed.
☐ Place foods to be cooked in the appropriate cooking dishes; refrigerate or set aside near stove.
☐ Garnish desserts.
☐ Assemble salads.
☐ Unmold and garnish molded salads.
☐ Set table and assemble centerpiece.

BEFORE SERVING
☐ Cook and heat foods as necessary.
☐ Arrange food on the table.

If your home is small, the food for a buffet-style meal does not have to be all in one place. The hot food may be near the stove or oven, the salad, bread and relishes could be in the dining area and the silver, napkins and beverages on a small table.

At the Table—The food is passed at the table and the guests help themselves.

From the Kitchen—This style of serving is best for a small number of guests. Appetizers may be passed in the living room. Prepare the dinner plates in the kitchen and bring them out two at a time. If there is room on the table for the bread and salad, all the better. Adjourn to the living room for dessert and coffee. Keep the dessert simple, such as cookies, candies or small pastries.

A Semi-Buffet—If a combination of any of these is easier for you, then do it. Appetizers can be served buffet-style, dinner may be served with the guests seated at the dining table and dessert served in the living room. Or the soup appetizer may be brought in from the kitchen, the dinner served from a buffet and dessert served in the living room.

A FINAL WORD

Your guests will enjoy the occasion if you're having a good time too. If your housekeeping, centerpiece or hors d'oeuvres are less than perfect, never mind. Relax and join the fun!

Marlene Sorosky

It wasn't until after Marlene Sorosky graduated from UCLA that she discovered the importance of entertaining. The social obligations of being an Army physician's wife kindled her interest in cooking and developed her abilities as a hostess. While living in France with her husband and their four children, Marlene attended cooking classes and began to experiment with recipes.

On her return to the United States she became involved with developing a cookbook and demonstrating cooking techniques. Her cooking and teaching talents worked well together and in 1973 she opened her own cooking school in suburban Los Angeles. Her most popular classes emphasize advance preparation of food for entertaining. This emphasis, Marlene finds, leads to a greater awareness of the taste of fine food and an appreciation of its visual delights. Best of all, good planning means her students learn to be guests at their own parties. So can you, because the best ideas and recipes developed for Marlene's classes form the basis for this book.

Freeze Now—Enjoy Later

Use this table as a reference for freezing and thawing the dishes made from recipes in this book or other cookbooks. For best results, wrap the foods to be frozen in sturdy freezer foil.

FOOD	HOW TO FREEZE	USE WITHIN	HOW TO THAW	PREPARATION
Hors d'Oeuvres Unbaked	Flash freeze, see page 5, on baking sheets. Remove and place in foil-lined boxes, plastic containers or plastic bags.	2 to 3 months.	Place on baking sheet. Thaw 1 to 2 hours at room temperature.	Bake according to recipe.
Baked	Same as above.	2 to 3 months.	Place on baking sheet. Thaw 1 to 2 hours at room temperature or reheat frozen.	Reheat at 375°F (190°C) until hot or according to recipe.
Dips & spreads	Must specify "may be frozen." Freeze in airtight containers.	1 to 2 months.	In refrigerator overnight.	Stir well. Serve cold or at room temperature.
Soups	In airtight containers.	4 to 6 months.	In refrigerator overnight or at room temperature several hours.	Reheat slowly on top of stove.
Stews, chili, meat in sauce	Line bowl with foil. Place meat and sauce in bowl. Be sure sauce covers all meat pieces. Cover with foil. Freeze until solid. Remove foil package from bowl. Return to freezer. May also be frozen in airtight containers.	3 months.	Remove foil. Place food in covered bowl or saucepan. Thaw overnight at room temperature, or on top of stove or in oven at low heat.	Reheat on top of stove or in oven.
Casseroles	Line baking dish with foil. Fill with casserole mixture. Cover with foil. Freeze until solid. Remove foil package from dish. Return to freezer. May also be frozen in baking dish.	3 months.	Remove foil. Place food in original baking dish. Cover. Thaw overnight at room temperature.	Bake according to recipe or reheat at 350°F (175°F) until heated through.
Breads Muffins & quick breads	Wrap in foil or plastic bags.	2 to 3 months.	Well-wrapped at room temperature 2 to 3 hours.	At room temperature or reheat wrapped in foil.
Yeast breads	Same as above.	9 months.	Same as above.	At room temperature.
Molds	Must specify "may be frozen." Freeze in the mold. Cover with plastic wrap and heavy foil.	2 weeks to 1 month.	In refrigerator overnight.	Unmold onto serving platter and refrigerate.
Cakes Unfrosted	Cakes do not freeze solid. To prevent crushing, freeze in covered plastic containers or tin boxes. May also be frozen wrapped in foil.	4 to 6 months.	Covered, at room temperature 3 to 4 hours.	Frost and serve according to recipe.
Frosted	Butter cream and whipped cream frostings freeze well. Flash freeze, see page 5, in cake container or bakery cake box.	1 to 2 months.	In refrigerator overnight.	Cold or at room temperature, according to recipe.
Pies	Chiffon and fruit pies freeze well. Custard pies do not. In box or plastic container tightly covered with foil.	2 months.	In refrigerator overnight.	Cold, warm or room temperature according to recipe.

FOOD	HOW TO FREEZE	USE WITHIN	HOW TO THAW	PREPARATION
Cookies	In tins, plastic containers or shoe boxes lined with foil.	3 to 6 months.	1 to 2 hours at room temperature.	At room temperature.
Pastry dough or cookie dough	Shape into flat balls. Wrap in plastic wrap and heavy foil.	4 to 6 months.	In refrigerator several hours.	Use according to recipe.
Pie Crusts Unbaked & rolled out	Roll dough into large circle to fit in pie plate. For more than one, separate with sheets of wax paper. Wrap securely in foil.	4 to 6 months.	In refrigerator several hours. Press into pie plate when completely thawed.	Baked filled or unfilled according to recipe.
Baked	In pie plate, covered with foil.	4 to 6 months.	In refrigerator 2 to 3 hours.	Use according to recipe.

Tips for Efficient Freezing

• Wrap foods to be frozen as tightly as possible. As foods freeze, any air left in the package draws moisture from the food, reducing its freshness.

• Label and date all packages before freezing. If foods are frozen too long, they will not spoil, but they will lose some of their moisture and flavor. It's also helpful to include thawing and cooking or reheating instructions on the label.

• **Flash freeze** means to freeze food uncovered until it is solid, then wrap it well and return it to the freezer. This technique applies to foods such as frosted cakes and hors d'oeuvres which might become damaged if wrapped before they are frozen.

• Undercook vegetables you plan to freeze. They will finish cooking when they are reheated.

• The flavors from garlic and cloves become stronger when frozen. The flavors of onions, salts and herbs diminish.

• Unwhipped whipping cream may be frozen. Thaw it in the refrigerator and whip it as needed.

• Food that was frozen before the party can be refrozen, but *do not refreeze raw foods.*

• Leftover buttermilk may be frozen in its cardboard container. Thaw it in the refrigerator and shake the container before using.

• To freeze leftover tomato paste, drop it by tablespoonfuls onto a baking sheet lined with wax paper. Flash freeze or freeze uncovered until each mound is solid. Remove mounds from the wax paper, place in plastic bags, and return them to the freezer. Use as needed.

MENU SUBSTITUTIONS

The recipes in this book are arranged according to menus designed for particular kinds of parties, but they are meant only as guides. Feel free to mix and match your favorite recipes and create your own menus.

If there is an item you don't like on the menu you have selected, browse through the book for a substitution. If you're having a Card Party, page 69, and you don't like cheese soup, serve Creamed Tomato Bisque, page 60, instead.

If you're having a crowd over for the Holiday Open House, page 80, you may find it easier to serve all cold food. Substitute the Holiday Cheese Log, page 114, for Apple-Liver Rumaki. To accommodate extra guests, add the Molded Avocado Pinwheel, page 112.

An Elegant Supper, page 75, calls for your choice of two soups. If soup does not fit into your buffet plans, substitute the Chicken Liver Brochettes, page 37.

SHAPING THE MENU TO FIT THE PARTY

Most of the recipes in this book serve eight to twelve. If you are having four to six guests, you can halve some of the recipes at a glance. But most recipes are better left alone. Instead of halving recipes, serve fewer dishes. Serve one vegetable instead of two. Leave out the salad and prepare only one dessert.

If you are going to have 20 to 30 guests, it will be easier to prepare two extra recipes successfully than to take a chance on doubling recipes. So make one or two extra appetizers, add a molded salad and bread or rolls, and thaw an extra cake or platter of cookies.

How To Make Sugar & Spice Grapes

You Will Need:

1 egg white
1/2 cup sugar
1 teaspoon cinnamon

1/2 teaspoon
    ground cardamom
1 lb. grapes

Sugar & Spice Grapes are an elegant garnish for a fruit or dessert platter. In a small bowl, beat the egg white until it's frothy. In another small bowl, mix the sugar, cinnamon and cardamom. Cut the bunches of grapes into small clusters. Holding the stem of a cluster, dip it into the egg white. Shake off the excess egg white and roll the grapes in the sugar mixture until they are coated. Refrigerate them on a rack until the coating is set or overnight. For an interesting variation, substitute cranberries for the grapes.

Coating Grapes with Sugar & Spice

How To Make Chocolate Strawberries

Dipping Strawberries in Chocolate

You Will Need:
15 to 20 large ripe strawberries with leaves on
6 oz. semisweet chocolate

Chocolate Strawberries are not difficult and they are a lovely way to end a fine dinner or luncheon. You can make them on the morning of your party or the day before. First wash and dry the strawberries, but do not remove their leaves. Line a baking sheet with wax paper. Melt the chocolate in the top of a double boiler over hot water. Holding each strawberry by the leaves, dip them into the melted chocolate and place them on the lined baking sheet. Refrigerate the strawberries until they are firm or overnight. Arrange them unwrapped on a pretty platter or place each one in a decorative bonbon wrapper.

How To Make Chocolate Leaves

You Will Need:

24 non-poisonous leaves such as camellia or rose leaves

4 oz. semisweet chocolate

Chocolate Leaves add a professional touch to both ordinary and elegant desserts. Wash and dry the leaves. Line a baking sheet with wax paper. Melt the chocolate in the top of a double boiler over hot water. With a table knife or a small spatula, spread the melted chocolate over the underside of the leaves. Place the leaves chocolate-side up on the lined baking sheet. Refrigerate them until the chocolate is firm. The chocolate-covered leaves may be frozen.

To remove the leaf from the chocolate, grasp the leaf's stem and pull gently. The chocolate and the leaf will separate. Discard the leaves and use the chocolate leaves to garnish desserts.

Coating a Leaf with Melted Chocolate

Removing Leaf from Hardened Chocolate.

How To Make a Vegetable Basket

You Will Need:

Ice Water
Radishes
Zucchini
Cucumber
Carrots
Turnip
Lettuce

Cauliflower
Broccoli
Green Beans
Cherry Tomatoes
Mushrooms
Dill Dip, page 117
A large wicker basket

Cutting Radish Tulips, Roses and Fans

Making Turnip Daisies

Slicing Fluted Vegetables

If the vegetable garnishes and dippers are kept in ice water until the basket is assembled, they may be made a day or two ahead.

Radish Fans provide splashes of color in a vegetable basket. Begin with a long thin radish. Place it on its side. With a sharp paring knife, make thin slices almost but not quite through the radish. Place the radish in ice water for at least one hour to let it fan out.

Radish Tulips bloom like the real thing in ice water. Select a large radish. Cut off the stem so the radish sits flat. Beginning at the top of the radish, cut 4 thin slices of peel almost to the bottom, making 4 petals. Place the radish in ice water to open.

Radish Roses are an intriguing variation. Choose a round radish. Cut a thin slice off the bottom and top. Make 8 cuts across the radish almost to

The Filled Basket

the bottom, cutting first through the middle, then through each half and finally through each quarter. Place the radish in ice water to open.

Fluted Vegetables in appealing and easy-to-handle shapes are a definite improvement on plain vegetable sticks. Cut carrots, zucchini and cucumbers in sticks or slices with a French-fry cutter.

Turnip Daisies will never be recognized as turnips! Slice the turnip 1/4-inch thick. Cut the daisies with a cookie cutter. Place a small carrot slice in the centers. A dab of Dill Dip on the back of carrot slices will hold them in place. Turnip Daisies garnish molds, poultry platters and vegetables.

To Assemble the Vegetable Relish Basket, line a large wicker basket with lettuce and fill it with uncooked cauliflower and broccoli flowerets, green beans, cherry tomatoes, mushrooms and decorative vegetables.

Outlining the Whale's Shape

Relieving the Pressure

Scooping out the Fruit

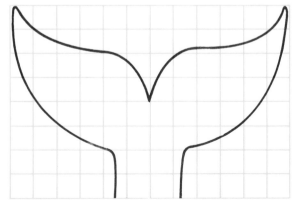

Completing the Whale

How To Make a Watermelon Whale

Watermelon Whale

To outline the shape of the whale, place the watermelon on a flat surface, stem-end toward you. The stem will be the nose. Enlarging the drawing on the facing page, make a pattern for the whale's tail. With a wooden skewer, outline the opening for the shell, then draw around the pattern of the tail.

To relieve the pressure inside the watermelon, use a sharp knife to cut an X through the top of the watermelon.

To make the shell, cut along the outline for the opening. Cut away the unwanted shell in pieces. Scoop out the watermelon fruit, leaving the shell about 1-inch thick. Reserve the watermelon fruit to add to the other fruit in the whale.

To complete the whale, outline the eyes and mouth with a wooden skewer. Cut out the eyes completely. Cut the mouth only halfway through the shell so the juices from the fruit will not run out. At this point, the whale may be covered with plastic wrap and refrigerated overnight. Before serving the whale, make several holes in the top of the head with a small skewer. Push dried flowers into the holes to resemble spouting water. Fill the whale with melon balls or pieces, berries, grapes or other fruit. Garnish with mint, if desired.

You Will Need:
1 large watermelon
Assorted fruit such as melon balls,
  berries and grapes
Dried flowers
Sprig of mint, if desired

How To Make a Luau Centerpiece

Making the Bark for the Trunk of a Palm Tree

You Will Need:

Ice Water	Green leaves such as Boston fern
2 florist's frogs	Assorted flowers
2 cucumbers	Citrus fruit wedges
2 green peppers	Purple grapes, if desired
1 pineapple	

Make the parts for this centerpiece two or three days ahead and store them in ice water to give the vegetables time to open. Be sure to have two florist's frogs on hand so the cucumber trees will stand steady.

Trunks of Palm Trees can be made quickly. Use a sharp paring knife to cut small gashes diagonally into the skin of 2 cucumbers to resemble bark. Make the cuts very thin and at least 1/2-inch long. Cut both ends off the cucumbers to make flat surfaces. Place the cucumbers in ice water for two or three days to allow the cuts to open.

Leaves for the Palm Trees will look more realistic on the trees than in your hand. To begin, remove the bottoms of 2 green peppers. Remove cores and seeds by cutting up into the peppers from the bottom, leaving the tops intact. Cut sections to resemble leaves, leaving them connected at the top. Make diagonal cuts along each side of the leaves but do not cut through the center of the leaves. Place the peppers in ice water for two or three days to allow leaves to open.

The Pineapple Hut has an open door to convey the feeling of hospitality. Cut the top leaves off the pineapple, leaving on any attractive lower leaves. Slice a piece off the bottom so the pineapple will sit flat. With a sharp knife, cut as much pineapple from the inside as possible, leaving a thin shell. Cut into the pineapple to make the side and top of a door, leaving one side of the door attached.

To Assemble the Scene, line the bottom of a large platter with green leaves such as Boston fern. Push the cucumber tree trunks onto florist's frogs and place them on the platter. Top each tree with green pepper leaves. Place the hut on the platter. Cover the roof with flowers or leaves, securing them with straight pins. Decorate the platter with assorted flowers and citrus fruit wedges. If desired, hang purple grapes from the palm trees to resemble coconuts.

Cutting the Leaves for the Palm Trees

Constructing the Pineapple Hut

The Assembled Scene

How To Make a Tomato Rose

You Will Need: 1 firm tomato

Peeling the Tomato

Rolling the Peel

Tomato Peel Roses give salad plates, serving platters or dinner plates a touch of color and a bit of artistry. They may be made a few hours ahead, placed on a wet paper towel in a covered container and refrigerated.

To peel the tomato, use a sharp paring knife. With the stem-end of the tomato down, begin peeling on the smooth end. Cut around the tomato in a spiral, making a continuous strip about 3/4-inch wide. Do not be concerned if the peel breaks at some points.

To form a rose, roll one end of the peel tightly to make the center. Loosely but carefully roll the remaining peel around the center. Broken pieces can be worked in. Secure the bottom of the rose with half a wooden pick.

Festive Fare

Adventures in dining unfold with these two creative menus. Send your friends a picturesque post card of Mexico or the South Pacific, asking them to join you for a fun-filled fiesta or luau!

One of my favorite party menus is the Mexican Fiesta. To set a Latin American mood, welcome your guests with refreshing Margaritas, page 150. Set a colorful table with a splashy table cloth and the Sombrero Salad as the centerpiece. Small clay pots filled with fresh or paper flowers and green and red chili peppers will give a festive touch. The novelty of Carne Asada is having your guests devise their own creations from your tempting display. Each guest puts meat, guacamole and condiments onto a steamed and buttered tortilla, and tops them with mildly spicy Salsa. Refreshing Frozen Lemon Cream, which you can make several weeks ahead, is a perfect ending to this zesty meal.

The Island Luau is a splendid tropical spread, flexible in variety and quantity. Bring the floral shores of the islands to the table by creating lush and leafy palm trees from cucumbers and green peppers, pages 12 to 13. Begin your party with Mai Tai Punch, page 156, a blend of juices, light rum and brandy. Then on to the Polynesian-style meal with glazed pork ribs, Beef Teriyaki or fried Won Ton Bows. Even those who thought they didn't like curry will compliment your Chicken & Shrimp Kaanipali—especially if it's served from a chafing dish or in scooped-out pineapple shells. Prepared up to two days in advance, only the final assembly needs to be done on the day of the party.

Kona Crunch Pie has toasted nuts baked into the crust and is topped with an incredibly smooth and rich coffee-chocolate filling. Lime Angel Pie, with its delicate meringue crust and divinely light lime filling, is a contrast in taste and texture to Kona Crunch Pie, so you can serve both pies at the same meal.

If you prefer to serve one large dessert for either the Fiesta or Luau, Lemon Snowball, page 85, captures the same festive spirit.

Mexican Fiesta
Chili Cheese Bites
Mexican Meatballs
Coconut Bananas
Sombrero Salad
Refried Beans
Carne Asada In Tortillas
Salsa
Guacamole Spread
Frozen Lemon Cream
Mexican Wedding Rings

Chili Cheese Bites

An easy hors d'oeuvre to introduce this festive dinner.

4 tablespoons butter or margarine	Dash salt
5 eggs	1 (4-oz.) can chopped green chilies
1/4 cup all-purpose flour	1/2 pint small curd cottage cheese (1 cup)
1/2 teaspoon baking powder	2 cups shredded Monterey Jack cheese

Preheat oven to 400°F (205°C). Melt butter or margarine in a 9-inch square pan in oven. Tip pan to coat bottom with melted butter or margarine. In a large bowl, beat eggs. Stir in flour, baking powder and salt. Add melted butter or margarine; set pan aside. Stir in chilies, cottage cheese and Jack cheese. Mix until blended. Turn batter into butter- or margarine-coated pan. Bake 15 minutes. Reduce heat to 350°F (175°C). Bake 30 to 35 minutes longer or until lightly browned. Cool slightly and cut into small squares. May be frozen; see freezing table, Baked Hors d'Oeuvres, page 4.

Before serving, reheat in a 400°F (205°C) oven 10 minutes or until hot. Makes 32 hors d'oeuvres.

Variations

The recipe may be doubled and baked in a 13" x 9" baking dish.

One (10-oz.) package frozen chopped spinach, thawed and drained well, may be added with the chilies.

Mexican Meatballs

A surprise in every bite!

Chili-Wine Sauce, see below
2 lbs. lean ground beef
2 slices white bread, cut in small cubes

1 egg
2 teaspoons chili powder
48 small green pimiento-stuffed olives

Chili-Wine Sauce:
1 (24-oz.) bottle red chili sauce
1/4 teaspoon garlic powder
1/4 teaspoon onion powder
1 teaspoon rosemary

1 teaspoon thyme
1 bay leaf
1 cup burgundy wine

Prepare Chili-Wine Sauce; set aside. Preheat oven to 350°F (175°C). In a large bowl, mix ground beef, bread cubes, egg and chili powder until blended. Shape into small balls. Insert an olive into the center of each ball, reshaping ball if necessary. Place on rack in broiler pan. Bake 12 to 15 minutes or until medium-rare. It is not necessary to turn meatballs. Do not overcook; they will continue to cook in the sauce. Add meatballs to Chili-Wine Sauce. May be refrigerated several days or frozen; see freezing table, Stews, page 4.

Before serving, bring to room temperature. Reheat on top of stove. Serve hot from a chafing dish with wooden picks. Makes 48 meatballs.

Chili-Wine Sauce:
In a medium saucepan, mix all ingredients and bring to a boil. Reduce heat and simmer 45 minutes, stirring occasionally. Remove bay leaf.

Coconut Bananas

Beautiful on any fruit platter.

4 bananas, peeled
4 tablespoons lemon juice

1 pint dairy sour cream
1-1/2 cups shredded coconut

Cut bananas into 1-inch pieces. Place lemon juice, sour cream and coconut in separate bowls. Dip banana pieces in lemon juice. Roll in sour cream and then in coconut, making sure all sides are coated. Cover with plastic wrap and refrigerate several hours or overnight. Makes about 24 pieces.

Turn the page and be welcomed to the Mexican Fiesta. The Sombrero Salad, page 20, contains assorted fruit. Mexican Wedding Rings, page 23, and Frozen Lemon Cream, page 23, are the delicious desserts. To top the tortillas, try Refried Beans, page 21, shown in the center; Carne Asada, page 21, in the chafing dish, and, in the relish tray, sliced onions, Guacamole Spread, page 22, and chopped tomatoes. Salsa, page 22, is at the bottom right. Blushing Sangria, page 150, makes a refreshing contrast and is shown in the top right corner.

Sombrero Salad   *Photo on page 18.*

The sombrero (Mexican hat) should be 24 inches in diameter. With a larger sombrero, use more fruit.

1 medium pineapple, cut in wedges;
  reserve top
1/2 small watermelon
1 cantaloupe
1/2 honeydew melon

Coconut Bananas, page 17
1 to 2 pints strawberries
Mint sprigs
Green and purple grapes
Fluffy Fruit Dressing, page 139, if desired

Place sombrero on a platter. Secure the top of the pineapple into the peak of the sombrero with skewers or turkey lacers. Line the base of a sombrero with plastic wrap. Cut watermelon, cantaloupe and honeydew melon into serving-size pieces. A fluted French fry cutter works exceptionally well. Place fruit attractively around the sombrero's base. Garnish with sprigs of mint. Using straight pins, hang small clusters of grapes at random from top of sombrero. If your refrigerator can accommodate it, assemble the salad a day ahead. Cover with damp paper towels and plastic wrap. Serve with Fluffy Fruit Dressing, if desired. Makes 8 servings.

How To Make Sombrero Salad

1/It will be easier to move the filled sombrero if you place it on a platter before filling it with fruit. Attach the pineapple leaves to the top of the sombrero with turkey lacers or metal skewers, pushing them down through the leaves and sombrero.

2/After lining the brim of the sombrero with plastic wrap, arrange the fruit neatly in the brim. Add sprigs of mint for garnish. Pin small clusters of grapes around the top of the sombrero with straight pins.

Refried Beans   *Photo on page 18.*

A favorite with every Mexican dish.

1-1/2 cups chopped onion	1/2 cup beer, fresh or flat
2 tomatoes, chopped	Salt and pepper to taste
3 tablespoons bacon drippings or vegetable oil	2 cups sharp shredded Cheddar cheese (8 oz.)
4 (1-lb. 1-oz.) cans refried beans	
3 tablespoons chopped fresh cilantro, if desired	

In a large skillet, sauté onion and tomatoes in drippings or oil until tender but not brown. Stir in beans, cilantro, if desired, and beer. Cook uncovered, stirring occasionally, until mixture has thickened and will not run when spooned onto a plate. Season to taste with salt and pepper. Stir in 1 cup of cheese. Place mixture in an 11" x 7" baking dish. Top with remaining cheese. Refrigerate or freeze; see freezing table, Casseroles, page 4.

Before reheating, bring beans to room temperature. Bake in a 400°F (205°C) oven 30 minutes, until hot and bubbly. Cool 15 minutes before serving. Makes 8 to 10 servings.

Carne Asada   *Photo on page 19.*

Tender slices of steak and tasty condiments rolled up in a steamed tortilla.

2 onions, sliced paper-thin or chopped	3 lbs. beef fillet or top sirloin, sliced very thin
3 or 4 tomatoes, chopped	Salt and pepper to taste
1 (4-oz.) can whole green chilies, sliced thin	4 tablespoons butter, margarine or vegetable oil
Guacamole Spread, page 22	1/4 lb. butter, room temperature
Salsa, page 22	
18 corn or flour tortillas, 6 or 8 inches in diameter	

Place onions, tomatoes, chilies, Guacamole Spread and Salsa in small bowls or on a divided platter. Refrigerate until ready to use. Make 2 stacks of 9 tortillas. Wrap each stack tightly in aluminum foil; set aside until ready to use.

Before serving, bake tortillas in a 425°F (220°C) oven 15 minutes or until heated through and steaming. Do not overbake or tortillas will break and fall apart. While tortillas are baking, season meat well with salt and pepper. Heat 4 tablespoons butter, margarine or oil in a large skillet. Sauté meat slices over high heat until lightly browned on the outside but still pink inside. Place in a chafing dish. Remove tortillas from oven and wrap in cloth napkins to keep warm. Discard bottom tortilla of each stack if they have become tough. Place on a warming tray or in a chafing dish over hot water, if desired. Place bowls or platter of vegetables, Guacamole Spread, Salsa and 1/4 pound butter on table. Let each guest spread butter on a tortilla, then top with a small portion of meat, desired vegetables and sauce. Roll up and eat with fingers. Makes 8 servings.

Salsa **Photo on page 19.**

Not too mild, not too spicy; it's a perfect relish for meats and omelettes.

2 medium tomatoes, unpeeled
2 garlic cloves, crushed
1/3 cup chopped onion

1 teaspoon salt
1/3 to 1/2 cup green chili salsa
2 tablespoons salsa jalapeña

Place whole tomatoes in a small shallow pan. Broil under medium heat or several inches from flame. Turn tomatoes on all sides until skins are blistered and burnt and tomatoes are cooked through, 10 to 15 minutes. Cool. Place tomatoes in a blender or food processor fitted with the metal blade. Add remaining ingredients and mix until blended. Refrigerate several hours before serving. May be stored in the refrigerator for several months. Makes 1 cup.

Guacamole Spread **Photo on page 18.**

Mexico's delicious contribution to the world of salads.

2 large avocados, pitted and peeled
2 tablespoons dairy sour cream
1/8 teaspoon garlic powder
1/4 teaspoon salt
1 teaspoon lemon or lime juice

1/2 (4-oz.) can chopped green chilies
  (about 1/3 cup)
Tabasco sauce to taste
1/2 small onion, chopped
1 small tomato, chopped

In a medium bowl or food processor fitted with the metal blade, mash avocado. Add sour cream, garlic powder, salt, lemon or lime juice, green chilies and Tabasco sauce. Stir in onion and tomato; mix well. If not serving immediately, place a piece of plastic wrap against the surface of the guacamole to prevent it from turning dark. May be refrigerated up to 2 days or frozen; see freezing table, Dips & Spreads, page 4. Makes about 2 cups.

Fruits will stay fresh when cut a day before serving if they are layered in a bowl with damp paper towels between each layer, covered with plastic wrap and refrigerated.

Frozen Lemon Cream   *Photo on page 18.*

Serve in delicate bowls or scooped-out lemon shells.

3 cups whipping cream (1-1/2 pints)
1/2 cup lemon juice
1-1/4 cups sugar

3 tablespoons grated lemon peel
Whipped cream, if desired
Mint leaves, if desired

In a large bowl, mix cream, lemon juice, sugar and lemon peel until blended. Pour into 8 small dishes which can be placed in the freezer. Cover with foil. Freeze overnight or up to 1 month.

Do not thaw before serving. If desired, garnish each serving with a rosette of whipped cream and a mint leaf. Makes 8 servings.

Mexican Wedding Rings   *Photo on page 19.*

Vary the shapes of these cookies by forming crescents, fingers or balls.

1/2 lb. butter or margarine,
   room temperature for mixer,
   cold and cut up for food processor
1/4 cup powdered sugar
1/8 teaspoon salt

2 teaspoons vanilla extract
2 cups all-purpose flour
1 cup chopped pecans (4 oz.)
Powdered sugar

In a large bowl or food processor fitted with the metal blade, cream butter or margarine and powdered sugar until light and fluffy. Add salt, vanilla, flour and pecans; blend. Divide dough into 4 equal portions. Wrap each portion in wax paper. Refrigerate until cold enough to shape. Preheat oven to 325°F (165°C). Remove 1 portion of dough at a time from refrigerator. Pinch off small pieces of cold dough. With hands, roll each piece into a narrow strip. Press ends together to form a small ring. Place on ungreased baking sheets. Bake 15 to 18 minutes. Remove from oven and immediately roll in powdered sugar. Cool on wire racks. May be frozen; see freezing table, Cookies, page 5. Makes about 48 cookies.

To color coconut, mix a few drops of food coloring with 2 tablespoons of water. Stir colored mixture into coconut, mixing well.

Island Luau
Won Ton Bows With Sweet & Sour Sauce
Beef Teriyaki
Mai Tai Mold
Island Spareribs
Chicken & Shrimp Kaanipali
Avocado Bread
Tropical Salad Bowl
Green Beans With Cashews
Lime Angel Pie
Kona Crunch Pie

Won Ton Bows With Sweet & Sour Sauce

If you use your wok, be sure to heat enough oil so you can fry several bows at once.

Sweet & Sour Sauce, see below
Small amount of water

1 (12-oz.) pkg. won ton skins (3-inch squares)
Oil for frying

Sweet & Sour Sauce:

4 tablespoons sugar
4 tablespoons white vinegar
4 tablespoons ketchup
1 cup water
2 tablespoons cornstarch

2 tablespoons water
1/2 cup chopped green pepper
3 tablespoons canned crushed pineapple, drained

Prepare Sweet & Sour Sauce; set aside. With your finger or a small brush, spread a 1/2-inch strip of water down the center of each won ton square. Crinkle the center together to form a bow shape; twist once to secure. Repeat with remaining squares. Pour oil about 1/2-inch deep into a large skillet. Heat to 400°F (205°C). Fry won tons in hot oil in a single layer until golden brown on each side. Drain on paper towels. May be frozen; see freezing table; Baked Hors d'Oeuvres, page 4. Bows will also keep up to 1 month in an airtight container at room temperature.

Before serving, reheat bows in a 400°F (205°C) oven 5 to 7 minutes or until hot; check frequently as bows burn easily. Serve with Sweet & Sour Sauce. Makes about 50 appetizers.

Sweet & Sour Sauce:
In a small saucepan, bring sugar, vinegar, ketchup and 1 cup water to a boil. In a small bowl, mix cornstarch and 2 tablespoons water until smooth. Add to sauce. Bring sauce to a boil, stirring until smooth and thick. Stir in green pepper and pineapple. Sauce may be frozen; see freezing table, Dips & Spreads, page 4. Serve warm.

Beef Teriyaki

To make this popular dish, you'll need 16 to 20 nine-inch wooden skewers.

1-1/2 lbs. top sirloin or flank steak	1/4 cup water
1/2 cup soy sauce	2 tablespoons vegetable oil
5 tablespoons brown sugar	1/2 teaspoon ground ginger

Have butcher slice beef into strips about 1/4-inch thick and 1-1/2-inches long. Place beef strips in a glass or plastic bowl. Mix remaining ingredients until blended. Pour over meat; stir well. Refrigerate overnight, turning meat occasionally. Several hours before cooking, place skewers in ice water to soak. This prevents them from burning and splitting while meat is cooking.

Before serving, thread beef strips accordion-style on skewers. Broil 3 to 4 minutes on each side or until nicely browned on the outside and pink inside. Makes 8 to 10 appetizer servings or 4 to 6 main-dish servings.

Variation

Chicken or pork may be substituted for beef.

How To Make
Won Ton Bows With Sweet & Sour Sauce

1/Use your finger or a small brush to spread water across the center of the won ton. Crimp the moistened center together to form a bow shape then twist once so the bow will hold its shape.

2/Fry bows in hot oil until they are golden brown on each side. Drain on paper towels before serving with Sweet & Sour Sauce.

Mai Tai Mold

Bottled Mai Tai mix adds the tropical flavor.

1 envelope unflavored gelatin
Dash salt
1/2 cup pineapple juice
1/2 cup sugar
3/4 cup bottled Mai Tai Mix, without alcohol

2 egg yolks, slightly beaten
2 egg whites, room temperature
2 tablespoons sugar
1/2 pint whipping cream (1 cup)
3 bananas, sliced

In a large saucepan, sprinkle gelatin and salt over pineapple juice. Let stand 5 minutes to soften. Add 1/2 cup sugar. Cook over moderate heat until sugar and gelatin are thoroughly dissolved and mixture just begins to boil. Stir in Mai Tai mix. Cool. Stir in egg yolks. Refrigerate until thickened and almost set. In a small bowl, beat egg whites until soft peaks form. Gradually add 2 tablespoons sugar; beat until stiff. Fold egg whites into thickened gelatin mixture. In a small bowl, whip cream. Fold whipped cream and bananas into gelatin mixture. Pour into a 6-cup mold. Refrigerate overnight or up to 2 days.

Unmold gelatin to serve. To unmold, run the tip of a table knife around the edges. Dip bottom of mold in warm water and invert onto platter. Makes 8 to 10 servings.

Island Spareribs

Hoisin sauce, also called Peking sauce, is available in the Oriental section of most supermarkets.

3 to 4 lbs. small pork spareribs
1/2 cup sugar

1/2 teaspoon salt
Island Marinade, see below

Island Marinade:
1 cup ketchup
1 tablespoon Hoisin sauce
1 garlic clove, crushed
1/3 cup brown sugar, firmly packed

1 tablespoon honey
1 tablespoon soy sauce
1/4 teaspoon ground ginger

Sprinkle ribs with sugar and salt. Let stand 1 hour. Preheat oven to 350°F (175°C). Place ribs on rack in roasting pan. Bake 1 hour. Prepare Island Marinade. Brush marinade on ribs. Bake 15 minutes. Turn ribs and brush with additional marinade. Bake 15 minutes more or until well-glazed. Serve immediately. May be frozen; see freezing table, Baked Hors d'Oeuvres, page 4.

Before serving spareribs, reheat in a 350°F (175°C) oven 10 minutes or until hot. Makes 8 to 10 servings.

Island Marinade:
Mix all ingredients in a small bowl until blended.

Chicken & Shrimp Kaanipali

Even if you use all chicken or all seafood, the flavor blend is superb!

2 lbs. chicken breasts, split
1 cup water
2 celery tops
1 onion, thinly sliced
1-1/2 teaspoons salt
2 cucumbers
1 green pepper

2 tablespoons butter or margarine
Kaanipali Sauce, see below
2 lbs. cooked large shrimp
4 to 5 cups cooked rice
Assorted condiments such as Peach Chutney,
    page 65, chopped peanuts, Toasted
    Coconut, see below, raisins and pineapple

Kaanipali Sauce:
2 tablespoons butter or margarine
1 medium onion, chopped
1 garlic clove, crushed
2 medium green apples, peeled, cored and
    coarsely chopped
2 medium tomatoes, peeled and chopped
2 tablespoons all-purpose flour

1/2 teaspoon thyme
Scant 1/2 teaspoon cinnamon
1 to 2 tablespoons curry powder
2 teaspoons salt
1 cup chicken broth
1/2 cup whipping cream
1/3 cup dry white wine

Preheat oven to 350°F (175°C). Place chicken breasts in a 13" x 9" baking dish. Add water, celery tops, onion and salt. Cut wax paper to cover baking dish. Butter one side of paper. Place paper over chicken, buttered-side down. Bake 30 to 40 minutes or until chicken is tender. Remove from oven and cool. Remove skin and bones from chicken. Cut meat into bite-size pieces; set aside. May be refrigerated up to 2 days. Peel and halve cucumbers. Remove seeds. Cut cucumbers into 2-inch-long pieces. Cut pieces into thin strips. Remove seeds from green pepper. Cut into thin strips about 2 inches long. Melt butter or margarine in a small skillet. Sauté cucumber and green pepper until slightly wilted but still crisp. Vegetable mixture may be refrigerated up to 2 days. Prepare Kaanipali Sauce.

Before serving, place chicken, shrimp, cucumber and green pepper together in a large saucepan. Gently stir in sauce. Cover and heat. Serve with rice and assorted condiments. Makes 8 to 10 servings.

Kaanipali Sauce:
In a medium saucepan, melt butter or margarine. Sauté onion, garlic, apple and tomato until soft. Stir in flour. Stir over low heat 2 minutes. Add thyme, cinnamon, curry powder, salt, broth, cream and wine. Simmer 5 minutes. May be refrigerated up to 2 days.

Toasted Coconut   *Photo on page 67.*

A condiment with Chicken & Shrimp Kaanipali, above, or Curried Seafood Salad, page 66.

1 to 2 cups shredded coconut

Preheat oven to 350°F (175°C). Spread shredded coconut on a baking sheet. Bake 10 to 15 minutes, stirring occasionally, until lightly browned. May be stored in freezer in an airtight container. Makes 1 to 2 cups.

Avocado Bread

Surprise your guests with a pale green loaf, rich in taste, texture and nutrition.

1 egg	1/2 teaspoon baking soda
1/2 cup mashed avocado, (1 small)	1/2 teaspoon baking powder
1/2 cup buttermilk	1/4 teaspoon salt
1/3 cup vegetable oil	3/4 cup chopped pecans (3 oz.)
2 cups all-purpose flour	Butter, room temperature
3/4 cup sugar	

Preheat oven to 350°F (175°C). Grease a 9" x 5" loaf pan; set aside. In a medium bowl or food processor fitted with the metal blade, mix egg, avocado, buttermilk and oil until blended. Add flour, sugar, baking soda, baking powder, salt and pecans. Mix only until blended; do not overmix. Pour batter into prepared pan. Bake 55 minutes to 1 hour, until wooden pick inserted in center comes out clean. Cool 10 minutes. Turn out of pan. May be frozen and reheated; see freezing table, Breads, page 4. Slice and serve warm with butter. Makes 1 loaf.

Variation

To make Avocado Muffins, pour batter into greased muffin cups, filling 2/3 full. Bake in a preheated 350°F (175°C) oven 25 to 30 minutes. Makes 12 muffins.

Tropical Salad Bowl

Papaya slices spark the salad while the seeds flavor the dressing.

2 heads romaine lettuce	Papaya Seed Dressing, see below
1 head Bibb lettuce	1 large avocado
1 papaya	

Papaya Seed Dressing:

1/2 cup sugar	1/2 cup vegetable oil
2 teaspoons salt	1/2 cup choppped onion
1/2 teaspoon dry mustard	2 tablespoons fresh papaya seeds
1/2 cup white vinegar	

Wash lettuce and shake off excess water. Tear into bite-size pieces. Wrap in paper towels, place in a plastic bag and refrigerate overnight to crisp.

Before serving salad, place lettuce in large bowl. Peel and slice papaya, reserving 2 tablespoons seeds for dressing. Prepare Papaya Seed Salad Dressing. Peel and slice avocado. Add papaya and avocado to greens and toss with salad dressing. Makes 12 servings.

Papaya Seed Salad Dressing:

Place all ingredients except papaya seeds into blender or food processor fitted with the metal blade. Blend; add papaya seeds and process only until they are the size of coarsely ground black pepper. May be refrigerated up to 3 days.

Green Beans With Cashews

Glamorize green beans this easy way.

2 lbs. fresh green beans
Boiling salted water
4 tablespoons butter or margarine
1 cup chopped onion

3/4 cup salted cashews (3 oz.)
1/2 teaspoon lemon juice
2 tablespoons chopped parsley
Salt and pepper to taste

Cut ends off beans. Cut beans in 2-inch pieces and place in a large saucepan with boiling salted water. Cover and cook until tender but still crisp, 7 to 10 minutes. Drain; rinse under cold water to stop cooking. May be refrigerated overnight.

Before serving beans, melt butter or margarine in a large skillet. Sauté onion until tender. Add green beans and cashews. Cook and stir until heated through. Stir in lemon juice and parsley. Season to taste with salt and pepper. Makes 8 servings.

Lime Angel Pie

Heavenly, light and delicious.

Meringue Crust, see below
4 egg yolks
1/8 teaspoon salt
1/2 cup sugar
1/4 cup lime juice

1 tablespoon grated lime peel
1/2 pint whipping cream (1 cup)
Green food coloring, if desired
1/2 pint whipping cream (1 cup), whipped
1 lime, sliced thin

Meringue Crust:
4 egg whites, room temperature
1/4 teaspoon cream of tartar

1 cup sugar

Prepare Meringue Crust; set aside. Beat egg yolks and salt in a medium bowl until light and fluffy. Stir in sugar, lime juice and peel. Place mixture in the top of a double boiler over boiling water. Stir constantly, until thickened and smooth, 8 to 10 minutes. Remove from heat. Cool. Beat 1/2 pint cream until stiff. Fold into lime mixture. Add a dash of green food coloring, if desired. Pour into Meringue Crust. Refrigerate several hours or overnight.

Before serving pie, garnish with additional whipped cream and lime slices. Makes 8 servings.

Meringue Crust:
Preheat oven to 275°F (135°C). Grease a 9-1/2- or 10-inch pie plate; set aside. In a large bowl, beat egg whites and cream of tartar until soft peaks form. Gradually add sugar 1 tablespoon at a time, beating until very stiff. Spoon meringue into prepared pie plate, mounding the sides up and over the edge. Bake 1 hour. Remove from oven and cool.

Kona Crunch Pie

Good to the last bite!

Macadamia Nut Pie Crust, see below
3/4 cup sugar
1 envelope unflavored gelatin
2 teaspoons instant coffee powder
2 tablespoons unsweetened cocoa powder
2 tablespoons coffee-flavored liqueur
1/2 teaspoon salt

1-1/2 cups milk
2 egg yolks, slightly beaten
2 egg whites, room temperature
1/4 teaspoon cream of tartar
1/2 pint whipping cream (1 cup)
Chocolate Leaves, page 7, if desired
1/4 cup chopped macadamia nuts, if desired

Macadamia Nut Pie Crust:
3/4 cup macadamia nuts
1/2 (11-oz.) pkg. pie crust mix
1/4 cup brown sugar, firmly packed

1 tablespoon water
1 teaspoon vanilla extract

Prepare Macadamia Nut Pie Crust; set aside. In the top of a double boiler, mix 1/2 cup sugar, gelatin, instant coffee powder, cocoa powder, liqueur and salt. Stir in milk and egg yolks. Stir constantly over boiling water until mixture thickens slightly and is very hot. Remove from heat. Refrigerate or stir over a bowl of ice water until mixture is cooled but not set. In a small bowl, beat egg whites with cream of tartar until soft peaks form. Gradually add remaining 1/4 cup sugar, beating until stiff. Fold into thickened gelatin mixture. Whip 1/2 cup cream. Refrigerate remaining 1/2 cup. Fold into gelatin mixture. Pour into baked pie crust. Chill several hours or overnight. May also be frozen; see freezing table, Pies, page 4.

Before serving pie, whip remaining cream. Spoon or pipe whipped cream around edge. Garnish with Chocolate Leaves and chopped nuts, if desired. Makes 8 servings.

Macadamia Nut Pie Crust:
Preheat oven to 350°F (175°C). Grease a 9-inch pie plate; set aside. Rub macadamia nuts in a tea towel to remove excess salt. Coarsely chop nuts. Place on a baking sheet. Bake 8 minutes, stirring occasionally and watching carefully because the nuts burn easily. Cool. Increase oven temperature to 375°F (190°C). In a medium bowl, combine pie crust mix, brown sugar and nuts. Add water and vanilla. Mix with a fork until blended. Press dough firmly against bottom and sides of prepared pie plate. Bake 15 minutes or until edges are lightly browned; cool.

Variation

When making the crust, 3/4 cup toasted chopped almonds may be substituted for toasted macadamia nuts.

Never fold whipped cream into a warm mixture—the warmth will deflate the cream. To hasten cooling of the warm mixture, place bowl with mixture in a large bowl or pan of ice water and stir until chilled.

Brunch Get-Togethers

Mid-morning entertaining is steadily growing more popular, and it is easy to see why. A brunch offers casual elegance quite different from a dinner party or luncheon. And it's an enjoyable way to bring friends together without worrying about pairing or numbers.

Each of the menus in this chapter includes a choice of main dishes, so you can select one or more, depending on the number of guests.

The Sunday Brunch is designed for simplicity. Puffed Pancakes are guaranteed to astonish your guests. The batter may be prepared the day before, but the pancakes must be baked and served immediately to be admired at their fullest height.

In the Festive Brunch, the recipes are somewhat more elaborate. They can be adapted easily for a crowd. The two quiches are extraordinary! My students have enjoyed serving Boursin Cheese Quiche for breakfast, lunch, dinner, midnight supper or any time in between. Crustless Crab Quiche is another versatile recipe. Without the crab, it's a delicious side dish with beef, poultry or fish. You can quickly whip up the quiche in your blender or food processor. As it bakes, the batter forms its own crust. Batter for both quiches may be made a day ahead and refrigerated. Each of the soufflés may be prepared a day in advance, so in the morning all you have to do is put it in the oven and serve it right out of the baking dish. The Chicken Liver Brochettes may be assembled a day ahead, brought to room temperature and broiled before serving. Any of these dishes served alone will make a delicious brunch. If you are having a crowd, prepare as many dishes as your oven will accommodate. As your guests arrive, don't forget to serve the frothy Special Ramos Fizz, page 151. It's a sure way of whetting their appetites.

A Family Affair is the most casual of the brunches. Surprise your family with Creamy Scrambled Eggs or either of the pancake variations. Keep French Toasted Muffins in your freezer to take out and bake whenever the mood strikes you. Company Hot Chocolate, page 149, goes with any breakfast and is a delicious way to start the day.

Sunday Brunch

Baked Grapefruit Alaska
Sausage Puffs
Apple Puffed Pancake or Puffed Pancake With Strawberries
Best Bran Muffins
Chocolate Chip Coffeecake

Baked Grapefruit Alaska

This low-calorie special is also a marvelous dessert.

3 medium grapefruit
1 (10- or 12-oz.) jar orange marmalade
4 egg whites, room temperature

1/4 cup granulated sugar
Powdered sugar

Cut each grapefruit in half. With a grapefruit knife, remove center core from each half. To remove membrane, cut around between the flesh and the pith to completely detach flesh from shell. Slip the knife down each side of membranes, between grapefruit sections. Remove all membranes and seeds, leaving flesh in grapefruit shell. Place on a baking sheet. Place marmalade in a small saucepan. Heat until warm. In a medium bowl, beat egg whites until soft peaks form. Slowly beat in granulated sugar 1 tablespoon at a time. Continue beating until stiff. Carefully fold in warm marmalade. Cover grapefruit in shells with meringue, bringing meringue to the edge of the shells. Filled shells may stand at room temperature 2 to 3 hours until ready to use.

Just before serving, preheat oven to 425°F (220°C). Bake grapefruit 8 to 9 minutes or until nicely browned. Sprinkle with powdered sugar and serve immediately. Makes 6 servings.

Sausage Puffs

Delightful cheese puffs spiced with hot sausage are great as an hors d'oeuvre or as a side dish with eggs.

1 (12-oz.) pkg. hot bulk sausage
1 lb. sharp Cheddar cheese, shredded

1 cup buttermilk biscuit mix
Spicy Mustard Sauce, page 123, if desired

Preheat oven to 350°F (175°C). In a medium bowl, mix sausage, cheese and biscuit mix until blended. Shape into walnut-size balls. Place on a rack in a shallow pan. Bake 35 to 45 minutes or until lightly browned. Serve immediately with Spicy Mustard Sauce, if desired. Or cool and freeze; see freezing table, Baked Hors d'Oeuvres, page 4. Makes 48 puffs.

How To Make Baked Grapefruit Alaska

1/After removing the center core from each grapefruit half, cut around all sides of each grapefruit section, between the fruit and the membranes on 2 sides and between the fruit and the shell on the third side. Remove all membranes, leaving the fruit sections.

2/Mound the marmalade meringue mixture on top of the grapefruit, completely covering the fruit and sealing the meringue to the edge of the shells.

Apple Puffed Pancake

Cinnamon and apples make it extra delicious!

6 eggs
1-1/2 cups milk
1 cup all-purpose flour
3 tablespoons granulated sugar
1 teaspoon vanilla extract

1/2 teaspoon salt
1/4 teaspoon cinnamon
1/4 lb. butter or margarine
2 apples, peeled and thinly sliced
2 to 3 tablespoons brown sugar

Preheat oven to 425°F (220°C). In a blender or large bowl, mix eggs, milk, flour, granulated sugar, vanilla, salt and cinnamon until blended. If using a mixer, batter will remain slightly lumpy. Melt butter or margarine in a 12-inch fluted porcelain quiche dish or a 13" x 9" baking dish in oven. Add apple slices to baking dish. Return to oven until butter or margarine sizzles. Do not let brown. Remove dish from oven and immediately pour batter over apples. Sprinkle with brown sugar. Bake in middle of oven 20 minutes or until puffed and brown. Serve immediately. Makes 6 to 8 servings.

Puffed Pancake With Strawberries

Absolutely spectacular!

6 eggs
1 cup milk
1/4 cup orange-flavored liqueur or orange juice
1/2 cup granulated sugar
1 cup all-purpose flour

1/4 teaspoon salt
1/4 lb. butter or margarine
Strawberry Sauce, see below
Powdered sugar, if desired
Dairy sour cream, if desired

Strawberry Sauce:
2 (10-oz.) pkgs. frozen strawberries in syrup
2 tablespoons orange-flavored liqueur or
  orange juice

In a blender or large bowl, mix eggs, milk, liqueur or orange juice, granulated sugar, flour and salt until blended. If using a mixer, batter will remain lumpy. Preheat oven to 425°F (220°C). Melt butter or margarine in a 13" x 9" baking dish in oven until it sizzles. Do not let brown. Remove baking dish from oven and immediately pour batter into sizzling butter or margarine. Bake in middle of oven 20 minutes or until puffed and brown. While pancake is baking, prepare Strawberry Sauce. Remove pancake from oven. Sprinkle with powdered sugar, if desired. Pancake falls quickly so serve immediately with warm Strawberry Sauce and sour cream, if desired. Makes 6 to 8 servings.

Strawberry Sauce:
Heat strawberries in a small saucepan until hot. Stir in liqueur or orange juice. Serve warm.

Best Bran Muffins

Two kinds of bran cereal make a muffin with a new taste.

1 cup 100% bran cereal	2 cups bran buds cereal
1/2 cup boiling water	3 cups all-purpose flour
1 cup sugar	2-1/2 teaspoons baking soda
1/4 lb. butter or margarine	1 teaspoon salt
2 eggs	1 cup golden raisins, if desired
2 cups buttermilk	Butter or margarine

Preheat oven to 375°F (190°C). Grease 2-1/2-inch muffin cups; set aside. Pour boiling water over 100% bran cereal and set aside to cool. In a large bowl, cream sugar and 1/4 pound butter or margarine. Add eggs 1 at a time, beating after each addition. Add buttermilk. Stir in soaked 100% bran cereal and bran buds cereal. In a separate bowl, sift flour, baking soda and salt. Stir into bran mixture. Stir in raisins, if desired. Spoon into prepared muffin cups, filling 3/4 full. Bake 20 minutes or until wooden pick inserted in center comes out clean. Serve warm with butter or margarine. Cooled muffins may be frozen; see freezing table, Breads, page 4. Makes 36 muffins.

Chocolate Chip Coffeecake

Cream cheese adds to the light texture.

Pecan Topping, see below	2 cups all-purpose flour
1/4 lb. butter or margarine, room temperature	1 teaspoon baking powder
1 (8-oz.) pkg. cream cheese, room temperature	1/2 teaspoon baking soda
1-1/4 cups sugar	1/4 teaspoon salt
2 eggs	1/4 cup cold milk
1 teaspoon vanilla extract	1 (6-oz.) pkg. chocolate chips (1 cup)

Pecan Topping:

1/4 cup sugar	1/4 cup chopped pecans
1 teaspoon cinnamon	

Preheat oven to 350°F (175°C). Grease a 9" x 3" springform pan; set aside. Prepare Pecan Topping; set aside. In a large bowl, cream butter or margarine, cream cheese and sugar. Add eggs 1 at a time, beating well after each addition. Add vanilla, flour, baking powder, baking soda and salt; mix well. Stir in cold milk and chocolate chips. Mixture will be very thick. Pour into prepared pan. Sprinkle with Pecan Topping. Bake 50 to 55 minutes or until wooden pick inserted in center comes out clean. Let cool 15 minutes. Remove outside ring from springform pan and cool cake completely. May be frozen; see freezing table, Cakes, page 4. Makes 12 servings.

Pecan Topping:

Mix all ingredients in a small bowl.

Festive Brunch
Chicken Liver Brochettes
Blintz Soufflé With Blueberry Syrup or Easy Cheese Soufflé
Marinated Fruit Salad
Boursin Cheese Quiche or Crustless Crab Quiche
Ruby Poached Pears
Lazy Oatmeal Cookies

Chicken Liver Brochettes

Sage-seasoned butter and twelve 5-inch skewers do wonders for chicken livers!

1 lb. chicken livers
4 tablespoons butter or margarine
3 tablespoons olive oil

24 small mushrooms
Seasoned Butter, see below
8 slices French bread

Seasoned Butter:
6 tablespoons butter
2 teaspoons ground sage

2 tablespoons chopped fresh parsley
2 tablespoons finely chopped onion

Wash and dry livers; cut large ones in half. In a skillet over moderately high heat, melt butter or margarine with olive oil. Sauté mushrooms on both sides until tender. Remove mushrooms with slotted spoon and set aside. Sauté livers in same skillet until brown, about 3 minutes. Remove livers from skillet. Prepare Seasoned Butter; set aside. Preheat oven to 400°F (205°C). Remove crusts from bread. Spread Seasoned Butter on both sides of bread using half the butter. Cut each slice into three 1-1/2-inch cubes. Place bread cubes on a baking sheet. Bake 20 minutes, turning several times until toasted. On 5-inch wooden skewers, alternate toasted bread cubes, mushrooms and chicken livers. Place on rack in broiler pan. Spoon remaining half of Seasoned Butter over top, covering livers and mushrooms. Broil 2 minutes or until butter is melted. It is not necessary to turn brochettes. Serve as an appetizer, side dish or main course. Makes 12 servings.

Seasoned Butter:
Blend all ingredients in a small bowl or food processor fitted with the metal blade.

Blintz Soufflé

This indescribably delicious soufflé may be assembled a day ahead and baked before serving.

1/4 lb. butter or margarine, softened
1/3 cup sugar
6 eggs
1-1/2 cups dairy sour cream
1/2 cup orange juice

1 cup all-purpose flour
2 teaspoons baking powder
Blintz Filling, see below
Dairy sour cream
Blueberry Syrup, see below, or assorted jams

Blintz Filling:
1 (8-oz.) pkg. cream cheese, cut up
1 pint small curd cottage cheese (2 cups)
2 egg yolks

1 tablespoon sugar
1 teaspoon vanilla extract

Preheat oven to 350°F (175°C). Butter a 13" x 9" baking dish; set aside. In a blender or large bowl, mix butter or margarine, sugar, eggs, sour cream, orange juice, flour and baking powder until blended. Pour half the batter into prepared baking dish. Prepare Blintz Filling. Drop filling by heaping spoonfuls over batter in baking dish. With a knife, spread filling evenly; it will mix slightly with the batter. Pour remaining batter over filling. Unbaked soufflé may be covered and refrigerated several hours or overnight until ready to use.

Before baking, bring soufflé to room temperature. Bake uncovered 50 to 60 minutes or until puffed and golden. Serve immediately with sour cream and Blueberry Syrup or assorted jams. Makes 8 servings.

Blintz Filling:
In a medium bowl or food processor fitted with the metal blade, combine all ingredients until blended.

Blueberry Syrup

Here's a breakfast syrup that doubles as an ice cream sauce.

1 (15-oz.) can blueberries in light syrup
1/2 cup light corn syrup
1/2 teaspoon lemon juice
Dash salt

Dash cinnamon
1 tablespoon cornstarch
1 tablespoon cold water

In a small saucepan, combine blueberries, corn syrup, lemon juice, salt and cinnamon. Place on medium heat. Mix cornstarch with water. Add to blueberry mixture and bring to a boil. Remove from heat and let stand 5 to 10 minutes. Serve warm. May be refrigerated and reheated. Makes 2 cups.

Easy Cheese Soufflé

Try this make-ahead soufflé for the easiest brunch yet!

1/4 lb. butter or margarine, room temperature
1 (8-oz.) jar sharp process cheese spread
10 slices white bread

6 eggs
2-1/2 cups milk

Grease a 13" x 9" baking dish; set aside. Cream butter or margarine and cheese spread until blended. Remove crusts from bread. Spread cheese mixture on one side of bread and place cheese-side down in prepared baking dish. Some of the slices may have to be cut to fit. Spread top side with remaining cheese mixture. With a sharp knife, cut bread into 1-inch squares. In a medium bowl, beat eggs slightly. Add milk; mix well. Pour over bread. Cover baking dish with foil. Refrigerate overnight. Before baking, let soufflé stand at room temperature 30 minutes. Preheat oven to 325°F (165°C). Uncover soufflé and bake 1 hour or until top is puffed and brown. Makes 8 servings.

Variation

Add 1 cup diced cooked ham or bacon on top of bread before adding egg mixture.

Marinated Fruit Salad

Refreshing and flavorful—vary the fruits with the season.

3 large apples
3 large navel oranges
1 small pineapple
1 small cantaloupe

Spiced Marinade, see below
1 (1-pint) box strawberries, sliced
Mint leaves

Spiced Marinade:
1/2 cup sugar
1 cup water
1/2 teaspoon lemon juice
2 cinnamon sticks

1/2 teaspoon whole cloves
1/2 teaspoon whole allspice
1/2 cup kirsch liqueur

Peel apples and cut into 3/4-inch chunks. Peel oranges and separate or cut into sections. Cut pineapple into small wedges. Cut cantaloupe into wedges or balls. You should have about 2 cups of each fruit. Place fruit in a large bowl. Prepare Spiced Marinade and pour over fruit. Cover and refrigerate several hours or overnight until ready to use.

Before serving, stir in strawberries and garnish with mint leaves. Makes 12 servings.

Spiced Marinade:

In a small saucepan, combine sugar, water, lemon juice and cinnamon sticks. Tie cloves and allspice in cheesecloth and add to mixture. Bring to a boil over moderate heat; lower heat. Cover and simmer 5 minutes. Remove from heat and cool. Remove cinnamon sticks and spice bag. Stir in kirsch.

Boursin Cheese Quiche

Start the pastry several hours ahead or prepare and freeze it for a quick quiche when needed.

Flaky Pastry, see below
1 cup shredded Swiss cheese (4 oz.)
1/4 cup chopped green onions
1/4 cup chopped ripe olives

1 small tomato, seeded and diced
3 eggs
1/2 cup whipping cream
1 (5-oz.) pkg. Boursin spice cheese

Flaky Pastry:
1-1/4 cups all-purpose flour
1/4 teaspoon salt
1/4 lb. plus 2 tablespoons butter, room
    temperature for mixer; cold and cut up for
    food processor

3 to 5 tablespoons ice water

Prepare Flaky Pastry. Preheat oven to 375°F (190°C). Sprinkle 3/4 cup Swiss cheese on bottom of pastry. Sprinkle green onions, olives and tomato over Swiss cheese. In a medium bowl, mix eggs, cream and Boursin cheese; pour over vegetables. Sprinkle with remaining 1/4 cup Swiss cheese. Bake on bottom shelf of oven 35 minutes or until puffed and golden brown. Let stand 5 minutes before cutting into wedges. Makes 8 servings.

Flaky Pastry:

In a medium bowl or food processor fitted with the metal blade, mix flour, salt and butter until crumbly. Add ice water; mix until dough is thoroughly moistened. Place on a flat surface and knead into a ball. Wrap in wax paper and refrigerate several hours or until cold enough to roll. On a lightly floured surface, roll out dough to fit into a 9-inch pie plate or an 11-inch quiche pan with a removable bottom. Pastry may be refrigerated in pan covered with foil up to 1 week or frozen. Bring to room temperature before filling.

Ruby Poached Pears

The ruby red adds dramatic color to your buffet table.

6 ripe pears
1 (3-oz.) pkg. strawberry-flavored gelatin
3/4 cup boiling water

1 cup ruby port wine
3 (2-inch) cinnamon sticks
6 whole cloves

Preheat oven to 350°F (175°C). Peel, core and halve pears. Place in a 13" x 9" baking dish, cut-side up. In a medium bowl, combine gelatin and boiling water. Stir until gelatin is dissolved. Stir in port wine, cinnamon sticks and cloves. Pour mixture over pears. Cover with foil. Bake 20 minutes; baste well. Bake another 20 minutes or until pears are tender. Remove from oven and let cool in syrup. May be refrigerated up to 3 days and reheated. Serve warm or cold. Makes 12 servings.

1/If you are using a food processor, the butter must be cold and cut into 16 pieces. Insert the metal blade in the bowl of the food processor. Place flour, salt and butter in the bowl. Mix until crumbly, 10 to 20 seconds. Do not overmix. There will be some large pieces of butter not completely mixed into dough.

2/With the machine turned off, add 3 tablespoons of ice water. For a flaky, tender pastry, process only until the dough is thoroughly moistened; do not process until the dough forms a ball. Add more water a spoonful at a time as needed. The dough has the right amount of water when you can pick up a small amount between your fingers and it holds together without crumbling.

How To Make Flaky Pastry For
Boursin Cheese Quiche

4/After the pastry has been fitted into the quiche pan, make a small ball from a piece of excess dough. Gently press the ball against the sides of the pastry to help it adhere to the pan. Dip the ball of dough into flour occasionally to prevent it from sticking to the pastry. Press a rolling pin over the rim of the pan to remove excess dough.

3/On a flat surface, knead the dough into a ball. Some pieces of butter will still be visible. Flatten the dough slightly and wrap in wax paper. Refrigerate at least 1 hour or more for easier rolling.

Crustless Crab Quiche

Three cheeses blend for exquisite flavor.

1/2 lb. fresh mushrooms, thinly sliced
2 tablespoons butter or margarine
4 eggs
1/2 pint dairy sour cream (1 cup)
1/2 pint small curd cottage cheese (1 cup)
1/2 cup grated Parmesan cheese
4 tablespoons all-purpose flour

1 teaspoon onion powder
1/4 teaspoon salt
4 drops Tabasco sauce
2 cups shredded Monterey Jack cheese
  (1/2 lb.)
6 oz. fresh or frozen crabmeat, thawed and
  well-drained

Preheat oven to 350°F (175°C). In a medium skillet, sauté mushrooms in butter or margarine until tender. Remove mushrooms with a slotted spoon and drain on paper towels. In a blender or food processor fitted with the metal blade, blend eggs, sour cream, cottage cheese, Parmesan cheese, flour, onion powder, salt and Tabasco sauce. Pour mixture into a large bowl. Stir in sautéed mushrooms, Jack cheese and crabmeat. Pour into a 9- or 10-inch porcelain quiche dish or a 9-1/2-inch deep-dish pie plate. Bake 45 minutes or until knife inserted near center comes out clean. Quiche should be puffed and golden brown. Let stand 5 minutes before cutting into wedges. Makes 8 servings.

Variation

Substitute 1/2 pound cooked ham for the crabmeat.

Lacy Oatmeal Cookies

These delicate cookies keep well if carefully stacked in a tightly covered coffee can.

2 cups rolled oats, quick or regular
1 cup brown sugar, firmly packed
2 teaspoons baking powder

1/4 lb. butter or margarine, melted
1 egg, beaten

Preheat oven to 350°F (175°C). Generously grease baking sheets; set aside. Place oats, brown sugar and baking powder in a medium bowl. Add butter or margarine to oat mixture. Stir in beaten egg; mix well. Drop batter by half-teaspoonfuls onto prepared baking sheets 3 inches apart. Bake 8 to 10 minutes. Let stand 1 minute before removing from baking sheet. They will become crisp as they cool. May be frozen. See freezing table, Cookies, page 5. Makes about 40 cookies.

Family Brunch
Potato Pancakes or Cottage Cheese Pancakes
Glazed Ham Steak
Orange Blossom French Toast or
Freezer French-Toasted Muffins
Prune Bread
Creamy Scrambled Eggs
Coffeecake Fruit Squares

Potato Pancakes

Swiss cheese makes these special and they reheat beautifully.

1 (8-oz.) pkg. cream cheese
2 eggs
3 tablespoons all-purpose flour
3/4 teaspoon salt
1/8 teaspoon pepper

1 tablespoon onion powder
2 cups shredded Swiss cheese (8 oz.)
2-1/2 lbs. baking potatoes
Vegetable oil for frying

In a large bowl, thoroughly mix cream cheese, eggs, flour, salt, pepper and onion powder. Beat until smooth. Stir in Swiss cheese. Peel and grate potatoes. Squeeze a handful at a time to remove excess moisture. Stir grated potatoes into cheese mixture. Form into thick 3-inch patties. Discard excess liquid. Pour enough oil into a large skillet to cover the bottom. Heat oil. Fry pancakes in hot oil over moderately high heat until lightly browned on each side. Drain on paper towels. Serve immediately or cool, wrap and refrigerate or freeze; see freezing table, Baked Hors d'Oeuvres, page 4.

To serve, reheat in a 350°F (175°C) oven 15 minutes or until hot. Makes 6 to 8 servings.

Cottage Cheese Pancakes

So light and fluffy you'll need butter to hold them down!

4 eggs, separated
1/4 cup all-purpose flour
1/4 cup small curd cottage cheese

1/4 cup dairy sour cream
Dash salt

In a medium bowl, beat egg yolks, flour, cottage cheese and sour cream until blended. In a small bowl, beat egg whites with a dash of salt until stiff. Gently fold egg whites into egg yolk mixture. Spoon onto a moderately hot, greased griddle, spreading each pancake to about a 4-inch diameter. When underside is brown, turn pancake over, flatten slightly with a spatula and cook until golden. Makes 6 to 8 servings.

Glazed Ham Steak

Orange slices add flavor and texture.

1 (1-1/2-lb.) ham steak, 1-inch thick
1 small orange, peeled
1/4 cup molasses
2 tablespoons water

1/4 cup orange juice
2 tablespoons sugar
1/8 teaspoon dry mustard
1/8 teaspoon ground cloves

Preheat oven to 375°F (190°C). Place ham steak in a shallow 11" x 7" baking dish. Cut orange into very thin slices. Place on top of ham. In a small bowl, combine molasses, water, orange juice, sugar, dry mustard and cloves. Pour over ham. Bake uncovered 30 minutes; baste occasionally. Cut into wedges. Serve with a slice or two of orange on each wedge. Makes 6 servings.

To get maximum volume from beaten egg whites, bring them to room temperature before beating.

Orange Blossom French Toast

Golden egg batter with a delicate orange flavor.

12 slices bread	1 tablespoon grated orange peel
6 egg yolks	1/4 teaspoon salt
1/2 cup half-and-half	1/4 cup butter, margarine or vegetable oil
1/3 cup orange juice	Orange Syrup, page 48

Lay bread slices out overnight to become dry. In a medium bowl, slightly beat egg yolks. Mix in half-and-half, orange juice, orange peel and salt. Dip bread in batter, turning to coat both sides. Heat butter, margarine or oil in a large skillet. Cook bread on both sides until golden. Serve with Orange Syrup. Makes 12 servings.

Freezer French-Toasted Muffins

Freezer to oven or toaster oven with no last-minute fuss.

3 eggs	6 English muffins, split in half
3/4 cup milk	Melted butter or margarine
1 tablespoon sugar	Jam or syrup, if desired
1/2 teaspoon vanilla extract	

In a small bowl, mix eggs, milk, sugar and vanilla until blended. Place muffins on a rimmed baking sheet. Slowly pour egg mixture over muffins, turning to coat both sides. Let stand 5 minutes or until all liquid is absorbed. Flash freeze or place in freezer uncovered until frozen. Place muffins in a plastic bag and return to freezer until ready to use.

To serve muffins, preheat oven to 425°F (220°C). Grease a rimmed baking sheet. Remove desired number of frozen muffins and brush each side with melted butter or margarine. Place on baking sheet cut-side down. Bake 10 minutes; turn slices over. Bake 5 minutes longer or until golden brown and toasted. Serve with jam or syrup, if desired. Makes 12 servings.

Prune Bread

Baked in coffee cans, it's fun and unusual.

1 egg
1 teaspoon vanilla extract
1 teaspoon baking soda
1-1/2 cups coarsely chopped pitted,
   dried prunes
1 cup boiling water

1 teaspoon instant coffee
1/2 cup honey
2-1/4 cups all-purpose flour
2/3 cup sugar
1 cup chopped walnuts (4 oz.)
Cream cheese, if desired

In a large bowl, mix egg, vanilla, baking soda, prunes, boiling water and instant coffee until blended. Cover and let mixture stand 20 minutes. Preheat oven to 350°F (175°C). Grease and flour two 1-pound coffee cans; set aside. Stir honey, flour, sugar and walnuts into prune mixture. Stir until blended. Pour batter into prepared cans, filling each half full. Bake 50 to 60 minutes or until wooden pick inserted in center comes out clean. Cool 10 minutes. Invert on rack to remove bread from cans. Before serving, slice into thin rounds. Serve with cream cheese, if desired. Makes 2 round loaves.

Variation

Bread may be baked in one 9" x 5" loaf pan.

Creamy Scrambled Eggs

Cream cheese and chives add enjoyable flavor and color.

8 eggs
1/4 cup milk
1/4 teaspoon salt
Dash pepper

2 tablespoons butter
1 (3-oz.) pkg. cream cheese with chives,
   cut in 1/2-inch cubes
Chopped parsley, if desired

In a medium bowl, beat eggs, milk, salt and pepper until just combined. Melt butter in a large skillet over low heat. Pour in egg mixture. Cook over low heat. As eggs begin to set on bottom, gently lift cooked portion with spatula, letting uncooked portion flow to bottom of pan. Drop cream cheese cubes on top of eggs. Cook until eggs are no longer runny and cheese is melted. Sprinkle with chopped parsley, if desired. Makes 4 or 5 servings.

Coffeecake Fruit Squares

Vary the pie filling to change the taste.

Cinnamon-Nut Topping, see below
1/2 lb. butter or margarine, room temperature
1-1/2 cups sugar
2 eggs
1 pint dairy sour cream
2 teaspoons baking soda

2 teaspoons baking powder
3-1/3 cups all-purpose flour
2 teaspoons vanilla extract
1 (21-oz.) can pie filling, blueberry, cherry or
   apple

Cinnamon-Nut Topping:
1/2 cup brown sugar, firmly packed
2 tablespoons all-purpose flour
1 tablespoon cinnamon

2 tablespoons butter, room temperature
1/2 cup chopped nuts

Preheat oven to 350°F (175°C). Grease a 13" x 9" baking dish; set aside. Prepare Cinnamon-Nut Topping; set aside. In a large bowl, cream butter or margarine and sugar. Add eggs 1 at a time, beating after each addition. Mix in sour cream. Add baking soda, baking powder, flour and vanilla. Mix until blended. Spread half the batter in prepared baking dish. Spread pie filling over batter in baking dish. Carefully spread remaining batter over pie filling. Sprinkle Cinnamon-Nut Topping over top of batter. Bake 60 to 70 minutes or until wooden pick inserted in center comes out clean. Cool and cut into pieces about 3 inches square. May be frozen; see freezing table, Cakes, page 4. Makes 15 servings.

Cinnamon-Nut Topping:
In a small bowl, mix all ingredients together until crumbly.

Orange Syrup

A fabulous topping for French toast, pancakes or waffles.

1 cup brown sugar, firmly packed
1/2 cup orange juice

2 tablespoons grated orange peel

Mix all ingredients in a small saucepan. Simmer over low heat 5 minutes. Serve warm. Store in refrigerator and reheat before serving. Makes 1 cup.

Luncheons

From ceremonial bridal showers to carefree picnics, luncheons are a pleasant change from our daily routine.

There is no limit to the kind of showers you can create. Bridal and kitchen showers are popular. Ask each guest to include a favorite recipe with her shower gift. With a cake recipe, someone might give a pan to bake it in, a wire whisk, a sifter or an elegant cake plate.

Gala Champagne Punch, page 152, or refreshing Strawberry Wine Punch, page 156, help celebrate the occasion. If you are having a large group, include a non-alcoholic beverage such as Island Fruit Punch, page 156. The highlight of the shower menu is a beautiful fish which doubles as a colorful centerpiece. Choose between delicious Salmon Mousse or irresistible Poached Salmon. The mousse may be prepared all year round because it uses canned salmon. However, when fresh salmon is in season, grab it! Either dish can be garnished with lemon slices or wedges, thin cucumber slices and ripe olives. Serve these fabulous fish with either or both Dill Sauce and Cucumber Sauce.

Cream Puff Swans are a no-fail conversation piece! They look harder to make than they are. The swans may be prepared and assembled weeks in advance if you freeze them in a very large, tall container. Do not freeze them filled without the necks; the necks break easily when inserted into hard ice cream. If you're short on freezer space, make the necks and bodies ahead of time and freeze them unassembled. Fill and assemble them the day of the party, and keep them frozen until serving time.

Some gatherings demand light, carefree fare. This is where the Card Party Luncheon comes in. You can choose from two main-dish salads, Salad Niçoise and Chinese Chicken Salad. The ingredients for either salad may be prepared a day or two in advance and the salad assembled several hours before the luncheon. Keep Velvet Cheese Soup and frozen Lucky Lemon Cake in the freezer until the day of the luncheon, and you've got a ready-made party!

The Celebration Picnic is perfect for toting or as an informal meal at home. Take it on a boat, to a sporting event or an open-air theater. You'll love its versatility, great taste and ease. Sandwiches made in pita bread are fun and fascinating. The hollow pocket of the bread holds more than the traditional sandwich. Preparing the sandwich fillings the night before improves their flavor and lightens your work. Create new flavors by mixing and matching the various fillings. If you're picnicking on a cold, nippy day, take along a thermos of Hot Spiced Rum Punch, page 155. Then get ready to roll out the blanket, spread out the food and sit down to a glorious meal.

Open-Face Sandwiches

Dainty and bite-size open-face sandwiches are perfect for a buffet. Although sandwiches are best when they are made a few hours before serving, most fillings may be made in advance and refrigerated.

Use any type of thin-sliced bread. One standard thin-sliced loaf of bread will make about 80 two-inch square sandwiches. For neater sandwiches, put the bread in the freezer a few days in advance. The day of the party, remove the crusts from the frozen bread with a sharp knife. To prevent the bread from becoming soggy, spread each slice with softened butter *before* spreading with the filling. Cut the sandwiches one at a time into squares, triangles, rounds or strips with a knife or cookie cutters. Arrange them on a platter. Cover the platter loosely with wax paper and then with a clean damp dish towel. Refrigerate the sandwiches until serving time. Just before serving, garnish each sandwich with an olive slice, a pimiento strip, a pecan half or a small sprig of watercress or parsley.

Pita Bread Sandwiches

One advantage of using versatile pita bread is you don't need knives, forks or even plates. This is worth considering when you're planning a picnic! Allow at least one whole pita bread for each person. Serve assorted salads, spreads and sandwich fillings in plastic storage containers. Cut each pita bread in half so that it opens to form a pocket. Let your guests help themselves and fill their pita bread with what they like best. For those who want to try a little of everything, cut the pita bread in quarters and fill each quarter with a different filling.

Champagne Shower
Fruited Chicken Salad Sandwiches
Avocado-Egg Sandwiches
Curried Sandwiches
Cucumber Sandwiches
Dressed-Up Peanut Butter Sandwiches
Coconut Tea Sandwiches
Salmon Mousse or Cold Poached Salmon
Cucumber Sauce
Dill Sauce
Marinated Zucchini Salad
Cream Puff Swans With Fudge Nut Sauce

Fruited Chicken Salad Sandwiches

A surprisingly compatible blend of flavors and textures.

1 cup finely chopped cooked chicken
1/2 cup finely chopped celery
1/2 cup finely chopped apple
1/3 cup crushed pineapple, well-drained
3 tablespoons mayonnaise
1/4 teaspoon salt
1/8 teaspoon white pepper

1 teaspoon lemon juice
1/4 teaspoon onion powder
Butter
8 slices bread
Unpeeled apple, thinly sliced
Crushed pineapple

Combine chicken, celery, 1/2 cup apple and 1/3 cup pineapple in a small bowl. Stir in mayonnaise, salt, pepper, lemon juice and onion powder. May be refrigerated overnight.

To serve, spread chicken mixture on buttered bread. Cut as desired. Garnish with apple slices and pineapple. Makes thirty-two 2-inch square sandwiches.

Avocado-Egg Sandwiches

If you thought the flavor of avocado couldn't be improved, try this recipe.

1 medium avocado
2 hard-cooked eggs
1 teaspoon lemon juice
1/2 teaspoon salt

1 teaspoon onion powder
8 slices thin-sliced bread
Pimiento

In a small bowl or food processor fitted with the metal blade, mash avocado and eggs. Stir in lemon juice, salt and onion powder. If mixture is not to be used immediately, place a piece of plastic wrap on the surface of the mixture to prevent it from turning dark. May be refrigerated overnight.

As close to serving time as possible, spread avocado mixture on bread. Cut as desired. Garnish with pimiento. Makes thirty-two 2-inch square sandwiches.

Curried Egg Sandwiches

Chopped olives perk up these pretty sandwiches.

3 hard-cooked eggs
1/4 cup mayonniase
1-1/2 teaspoon curry powder
3 tablespoons chopped ripe olives

Dash salt
Butter
10 slices thin-sliced bread
Sliced ripe olives

In a small bowl or food processor fitted with the metal blade, chop eggs very fine. Add mayonnaise, curry powder, chopped ripe olives and salt. Mix until blended. May be refrigerated overnight.

Spread egg mixture on buttered bread. Cut as desired. Garnish with olive slices. Makes forty 2-inch square sandwiches.

To determine how much a mold will hold, fill a measuring cup full of water. Pour the water into the mold and repeat until the mold is filled. The number of cups of water indicates the cup-size of the mold.

Cucumber Sandwiches

Garnish popular cucumber sandwiches with a tasty cheese and anchovy topping.

1 thin cucumber, unpeeled
8 slices thin-sliced bread
1 to 2 tablespoons mayonnaise
3 tablespoons cream cheese (1-1/2 oz.)

1/4 cup blue cheese (1 oz.)
2 tablespoons half-and-half
1/2 teaspoon anchovy paste
Parsley sprigs

Slice cucumber very thin. Cut bread into 2-inch rounds, 2 rounds to a slice. Spread rounds with mayonnaise. Place a slice of cucumber on each round. In a small bowl, combine cream cheese, blue cheese, half-and-half and anchovy paste. Pipe or mound cream cheese mixture on each slice of cucumber. Garnish with a tiny sprig of parsley. Makes sixteen 2-inch square sandwiches.

Dressed-Up Peanut Butter Sandwiches

Peanut butter shows its versatility.

1/2 cup peanut butter
2 tablespoons honey

1/4 cup raisins or chopped dates
10 slices pumpernickel party rounds

Mix peanut butter, honey and raisins or dates. Spread on bread rounds. Makes ten 2-inch square sandwiches.

Coconut Tea Sandwiches

Spread on black bread for a real taste treat.

1 (8-oz.) pkg. cream cheese, room temperature
10 slices black bread, very thinly sliced
1/2 cup shredded coconut

1/2 cup chopped nuts (2 oz.)
20 small strawberries, halved

In a small bowl, beat cream cheese until fluffy. Spread on bread. Top with coconut and nuts. Cut as desired. Garnish each sandwich with a strawberry half. Makes forty 2-inch square sandwiches.

Salmon Mousse

Serve this molded showpiece when you're fishing for compliments.

1/2 cup cold water
2 envelopes unflavored gelatin
1 cup boiling water
1 cup mayonnaise
2 tablespoons lemon juice
3 tablespoons finely chopped onion
1 teaspoon Tabasco sauce
1/2 teaspoon paprika
1 teaspoon salt

2 teaspoons capers, rinsed and chopped,
   if desired
2 (15-1/2-oz.) cans salmon, drained or
   1-1/2 lbs. poached fresh salmon
1/2 pint whipping cream
Garnishes such as cucumber slices, pimiento,
   celery slices, ripe olives and lemon wedges
Cucumber Sauce, see below, or
   Dill Sauce, page 56

Oil a 6-cup mold; set aside. Place cold water in a large bowl. Sprinkle gelatin over water and let stand 5 minutes to soften. Pour boiling water over; stir until gelatin is dissolved. Stir in mayonnaise, lemon juice, onion, Tabasco sauce, paprika, salt and capers, if desired. Remove skin and bones from salmon; discard. Place salmon meat in a small bowl. Flake well or chop fine. Stir salmon into gelatin mixture. Whip cream until soft peaks form; fold into salmon mixture. Pour into prepared mold. Cover with plastic wrap and refrigerate until set or up to 2 days. May be frozen up to 2 weeks; see freezing table, Molds, page 4.

To unmold mousse, run the tip of a table knife around the edges, dip bottom of mold in warm water and invert onto platter. Garnish with cucumber slices, pimiento, celery slices, ripe olives and lemon wedges. Serve with Cucumber Sauce or Dill Sauce. Makes 8 to 10 servings.

Cucumber Sauce

Perfect with Salmon Mousse, see above, or Cold Poached Salmon, page 56.

1 very large or 2 medium cucumbers
1 cup dairy sour cream
1/2 teaspoon salt

1 tablespoon sweet pickle relish
1 tablespoon plus 1 teaspoon white vinegar
1 teaspoon sugar, if desired

Peel cucumbers; discard seeds. Shred cucumber using hand grater or shredder blade of food processor. Place shredded cucumbers in a strainer and let stand 30 minutes. Squeeze out all excess juice. Place cucumber in a small bowl. Stir in remaining ingredients until blended. May be refrigerated up to 2 days. Makes 1-1/2 cups.

Cold Poached Salmon

A great catch for your buffet!

1 (3- to 5-lb.) fresh salmon, head and center
    bones removed (allow 1/2 lb. per person)
4 cups water
2 cups dry white wine
1 large onion, sliced
2 stalks celery with tops, sliced

2 carrots, sliced
1 tablespoon black peppercorns
Cucumber Sauce, page 55, or
    Dill Sauce, see below
4 parsley sprigs
2 slices lemon

Wrap fish in cheesecloth, leaving ends long enough to hang over edge of pot and serve as handles for lifting fish; set aside. In fish poacher or roasting pan, combine water, wine, onion, celery, carrots and peppercorns. Bring to a boil. Lower heat. Cover and simmer 30 minutes to make stock. Gently lower fish into stock. Cover and cook over low heat 20 to 35 minutes, 7 minutes per pound. Do not let stock boil; it should barely simmer. Fish is done when it loses its transparency and flakes easily. Remove from heat. Cool fish in stock. When cool, lift fish out, using ends of cloth as handles and gently roll onto platter. Remove cheesecloth and peel off skin. Chill fish several hours or overnight.

Before serving, prepare Cucumber Sauce or Dill Sauce. Serve sauce in small bowls or spread over salmon as a topping. Garnish platter with parsley and lemon slices. Makes 6 to 10 servings.

Dill Sauce

A great dip for raw vegetables, too.

1/2 pint dairy sour cream (1 cup)
1-1/2 tablespoons white vinegar
1-1/2 tablespoons Dijon-style mustard

3 tablespoons brown sugar
2 to 3 tablespoons chopped fresh dill or
    2 teaspoons dry dill

Mix all ingredients in a small bowl. Refrigerate several hours to blend flavors. May be refrigerated up to 1 week. Makes 1-1/4 cups.

Marinated Zucchini Salad

Marinated overnight, zucchini takes on a zesty flavor.

1-1/2 cups beef broth
8 medium zucchini
16 cherry tomatoes

Zesty Marinade, see below
Boston or red leaf lettuce
1 (4-oz.) can sliced ripe olives

Zesty Marinade:
1/2 cup olive oil or vegetable oil
1/3 cup wine vinegar
3 teaspoons Dijon-style mustard
3/4 teaspoon salt
1/4 teaspoon pepper

3 tablespoons chopped green pepper
3 tablespoons chopped green onion
3 tablespoons chopped parsley
1 teaspoon dry tarragon

In a wide saucepan, bring broth to a boil. Add whole zucchini. Return to a boil. Cover and cook 8 minutes or until zucchini are barely tender when pierced with a fork. Do not overcook; they will soften as they marinate. Prepare Zesty Marinade. Remove zucchini from heat and immediately plunge them into ice water to stop cooking. Drain, cool and cut lengthwise into eighths. Place in a 13" x 9" glass baking dish. Add tomatoes. Pour marinade over. Cover with plastic wrap and refrigerate overnight.

To serve salad, line a large platter or individual salad plates with lettuce leaves. Place zucchini on top. Cut tomatoes in half and arrange around zucchini. Garnish with sliced olives. Drizzle additional marinade over. Makes 8 servings.

Zesty Marinade:
In a blender or food processor fitted with the metal blade, combine oil, vinegar, mustard, salt and pepper until blended. Place in a small bowl. Stir in green pepper, green onion, parsley and tarragon.

Fudge Nut Sauce

It hardens on the ice cream like the topping on a dipped cone.

1/2 lb. butter or margarine
1 (12-oz.) pkg. chocolate chips (2 cups)

1 cup coarsely chopped walnuts or pecans
   (6 to 8 oz.)

In a double boiler over hot water, melt butter or margarine and chocolate chips, stirring until smooth. Stir in nuts. Serve hot. May be refrigerated and reheated. Makes 2 cups.

Cream Puff Swans

Milk instead of water in the batter accounts for the soft texture of the frozen swans.

Cream Puff Sections, see below
1 qt. plus 1 pint vanilla ice cream

Fudge Nut Sauce, page 57

Cream Puff Sections:

1 cup milk
1/4 lb. butter or margarine, cut
1 teaspoon sugar

Dash salt
1 cup all-purpose flour
4 large eggs

Prepare Cream Puff Sections. Cut 1/3 off top of rounded puff. Fill the bottom with a scoop of ice cream; insert a neck into 1 end. Cut top piece in half for wings. Place wings, slanting upwards slightly onto each side of ice cream. Repeat with remaining Cream Puff Sections. Freeze until ready to serve. Swans may be kept frozen for several weeks in a large airtight container.

Remove swans from freezer 10 minutes before serving. Serve with Fudge Nut Sauce. Makes 10 swans.

Cream Puff Sections:

In a medium saucepan over moderately high heat, heat milk, butter or margarine, sugar and salt only until mixture begins to boil and butter or margarine is melted. Remove from heat and immediately pour in flour. Stir vigorously until dough forms a ball and leaves the sides of the pan. Return to heat and stir 1 to 2 minutes to dry out dough. Remove from heat. Make a well in center of dough and add eggs 1 at a time, beating after each addition. After the last egg, beat a minute longer, until dough is smooth and shiny. Preheat oven to 400°F (205°C). Lightly grease 2 baking sheets. Fit a pastry bag with a 5/8-inch rose tip (#124). Fill bag with about 1/4 of the batter. Pipe out 12 to 14 swans' necks on 1 baking sheet, as pictured, making extra necks to allow for breakage. To make bodies, drop heaping tablespoons of dough onto second baking sheet, making ten 2-1/2-inch oval mounds. Leave room between mounds for expansion. Bake bodies 25 to 35 minutes or until golden. Cool in oven 1 hour with door ajar. Bake necks with bodies but remove from oven after 10 minutes or when underside is golden. Necks and bodies may be frozen in an airtight container. Let stand at room temperature 1 hour before filling.

Variation

1 pint whipping cream, whipped and sweetened, may be substituted for the ice cream. Fill swans and refrigerate only 1 to 2 hours before serving.

1/Fill a pastry bag fitted with a 5/8-inch rose tip, with about one-fourth of the batter. On a lightly greased baking sheet, pipe out 13 to 14 S-shaped swans' necks. You'll have 2 to 4 extra necks to allow for breakage. On another lightly greased baking sheet, make 10 bodies by dropping heaping tablespoons of dough to form oval mounds. Mounds should be about 2-1/2 inches long. Necks and bodies may be frozen after baking. Thaw at room temperature 1 hour before filling.

2/Cut off the top third of each baked body. Cut the top in half to make the wings.

How To Make Cream Puff Swans

3/Fill the bottom of the puff with a scoop of ice cream. Insert one end of a neck into the ice cream at one end of the body.

4/Press a wing into the ice cream on each side of the body. Slant the wings slightly upward. Swans may be served immediately with Fudge Nut Sauce or frozen in an airtight container.

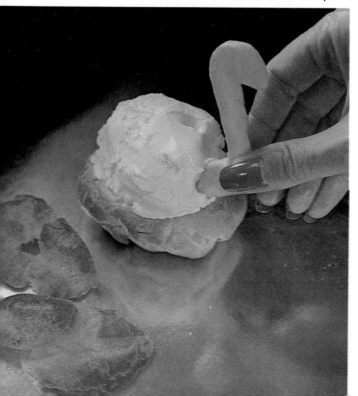

Celebration Picnic
Creamed Tomato Bisque
Middle Eastern Relish
Pita Bread
Cold Meat Salad
Eggplant Salad
Nature's Tuna Salad
Hummus Spread
Fruit Kabobs
Caramel Graham Cracker Cookies

Creamed Tomato Bisque

Pour hot or cold bisque into a thermos for an elegant picnic.

1/4 lb. butter or margarine
1 cup chopped celery
1 cup chopped onion
1/2 cup chopped carrots
1/3 cup all-purpose flour
2 (1-lb. 12-oz.) cans whole tomatoes,
   drained and chopped
2 teaspoons sugar
1 teaspoon basil

1 teaspoon marjoram
1 bay leaf
4 cups chicken broth
1 pint whipping cream (2 cups)
1/2 teaspoon paprika
1/2 teaspoon curry powder
1/4 teaspoon white pepper
Salt to taste

Melt butter or margarine in a large saucepan. Sauté celery, onion and carrots until tender. Stir in flour. Cook 2 minutes, stirring constantly. Add tomatoes, sugar, basil, marjoram, bay leaf and chicken broth. Cover and simmer 30 minutes, stirring occasionally. Discard bay leaf. Puree 1/3 of the mixture at a time in blender. Add cream, paprika, curry powder and pepper. Stir to blend. Add salt to taste. Serve hot or cold. May be refrigerated several days or frozen; see freezing table, Soups, page 4. Makes 8 servings.

Middle Eastern Relish

Serve this flavorful relish with luncheon meats and cheeses.

1/2 cucumber
Salt
1/2 small red onion, chopped
1/2 small green pepper, chopped
1 tomato, chopped
2 tablespoons chopped parsley
2 tablespoons white vinegar
1 tablespoon olive oil

1 garlic clove, crushed
1/2 teaspoon sugar
1/4 teaspoon salt
Dash pepper
1 tablespoon chopped fresh mint or
    1 teaspoon dry mint
1/3 cup crumbled feta cheese (3 oz.),
    if desired

Chop cucumber; salt lightly. Let stand in strainer 1 hour to drain. In a medium bowl, mix cucumber with remaining ingredients. Refrigerate several hours before serving or up to 2 days. Makes 2 cups.

How To Make Creamed Tomato Bisque

1/After simmering the vegetables in chicken broth for 30 minutes, puree one-third of the mixture in the blender. Remove pureed mixture from the blender. Repeat until all the broth and vegetables are pureed.

2/Stir in remaining ingredients until blended. The bisque may be served hot or cold.

Cold Meat Salad

A great way to use leftover meat. Mix it up tonight for tomorrow's picnic.

1/2 cup chopped green onions
1 cup sliced celery
1/2 cup coarsely chopped walnuts (2 oz.)
1/2 (10-oz.) pkg. frozen peas

2 cups diced cooked ham, beef, chicken or
   turkey
1/2 cup mayonnaise
2 teaspoons prepared mustard

Mix all ingredients in a medium bowl. Toss well. Refrigerate several hours or overnight. Makes 4 cups.

Eggplant Salad

A popular hors d'oeuvre to spread on crackers or triangles of pita bread.

1 large eggplant
1/2 to 3/4 cup olive oil
1 cup chopped onion
1 cup chopped celery
1 cup chopped green pepper

1 cup tomato puree (8 oz.)
1/2 cup chopped black olives
1/3 cup red wine vinegar
2 tablespoons sugar
1-1/2 teaspoons salt

Cut unpeeled eggplant into small cubes. In a large skillet, heat 1/2 cup olive oil over moderately high heat. Sauté eggplant, turning and stirring until nicely browned, about 10 minutes. Add onion, celery and green pepper. Cook and stir until vegetables are crisp-tender, adding more oil, if necessary. Stir in tomato puree, olives, vinegar, sugar and salt. Simmer uncovered 10 minutes, stirring occasionally. Remove from heat. Cool and refrigerate several hours or overnight. May be refrigerated up to 1 week or frozen. Makes about 4 cups.

Nature's Tuna Salad

For a light and pretty meal, fill a tomato with this nutritious salad.

1 (12-1/2 oz.) can tuna, drained
1 cup chopped celery
1 cup alfalfa sprouts
2 hard-cooked eggs, chopped
1/2 cup mayonnaise

1 cup shredded carrots
2/3 cup chopped green onion
1/2 cup chopped cucumber
2 teaspoons lemon juice
3 tablespoons pickle relish

Place tuna in a medium bowl; flake. Mix in remaining ingredients. May be refrigerated overnight. Makes 4 cups.

Hummus Spread

Sesame seed paste, or sesame tahini, can be purchased from gourmet shops.

1/2 cup chopped parsley
1 garlic clove, minced
1/2 teaspoon salt

3 tablespoons sesame seed paste
4 tablespoons lemon juice
1 (15-1/2-oz.) can garbanzo beans, drained

Place all ingredients in a blender or food processor fitted with the metal blade. Process until smooth. Refrigerate several hours before serving. May be stored in refrigerator up to 1 month. Serve cold as a dip or spread. Makes 1 cup.

Fruit Kabobs

Citrus juice marinade keeps the fruit fresh. Don't forget to check your supply of skewers.

1/2 cup sugar
1/4 cup water
1/4 cup lemon juice
1/4 cup orange juice
2 apples, unpeeled

2 pears, unpeeled
1 (8-1/4-oz.) can pineapple chunks, drained
1 (11-oz.) can mandarin orange segments,
    drained

Mix sugar, water, lemon juice and orange juice in a large bowl. Core apples and pears. Cut into 1-1/2-inch pieces. Add to marinade. Toss gently to coat all fruit. Add pineapple chunks and orange segments. Cover and refrigerate several hours or overnight.

To serve kabobs, drain fruit and thread on fourteen to sixteen 6-inch wooden skewers. Makes 14 to 16 servings.

Variation

Berries, peaches or melons may be substituted in season. If using berries, do not marinate.

Caramel Graham Cracker Cookies

The young at heart as well as the young in years love these, so keep extra in your freezer.

24 graham cracker squares
1/2 lb. butter or margarine

1 cup brown sugar, firmly packed
1-1/2 cups chopped walnuts or pecans (6 oz.)

Preheat oven to 350°F (175°C). Place all the graham crackers on an ungreased large rimmed baking sheet. In a small heavy saucepan over moderate heat, melt butter or margarine and brown sugar. Bring to a boil and stir constantly while boiling for 5 minutes. Pour carmelized mixture evenly over graham crackers. Sprinkle top with nuts. Bake 10 minutes. Cool 10 minutes. Cut in between each square and then through the middle, making rectangular bars. Cool completely. May be frozen; see freezing table, Cookies, page 5. Makes 48 cookies.

A Special Occasion
Raspberry-Wine Fruit Soup
High Hat Popovers
Peach Chutney
Curried Seafood Salad
Party Bombe With Frosted Flowers

Raspberry-Wine Fruit Soup

A scooped out watermelon half makes a beautiful serving bowl for this refreshing soup.

2 (10-oz.) pkgs. frozen raspberries in syrup,
   thawed
2 (11-oz.) cans mandarin orange segments
1 cup orange juice
1/2 cup burgundy wine

1/2 cup lemon juice
2 cups pink Chablis wine
1/4 cup quick-cooking tapioca
2 tablespoons kirsch liqueur

Drain juice from raspberries and orange segments into a 3-quart saucepan; set fruit aside. Add orange juice, burgundy wine, lemon juice, Chablis wine and tapioca to saucepan. Stir occasionally over moderately high heat until mixture comes to a full boil. Remove from heat and cool 20 minutes. Add kirsch and reserved fruit. Refrigerate overnight or up to 2 days. May be frozen; see freezing table, Soups, page 4.

Serve cold soup in chilled soup cups, wine goblets or in cantaloupe halves. Makes 8 to 10 servings.

High Hat Popovers

A food processor doesn't beat in enough air for desired lightness, so use your blender or mixer.

2 eggs
1 cup milk
1 cup all-purpose flour

1 teaspoon salt
2 tablespoons butter or margarine
Butter

In a blender or medium bowl, mix eggs, milk, flour and salt until smooth. Refrigerate batter until ready to use or up to 2 days.

Before serving, preheat oven to 425°F (220°C). Grease twelve 2-1/2-inch muffin cups. Place 1/2 teaspoon butter or margarine in each cup and heat in oven until butter sizzles. Pour batter into cups filling each 1/2 to 2/3 full. Bake 25 to 30 minutes or until popovers are puffed and brown. Do not peak. Serve immediately with butter. Makes 12 popovers.

Peach Chutney *Photo on page 67.*

A wonderful condiment to serve with lamb and pork.

1 (29-oz.) can sliced peaches
2 cups brown sugar, firmly packed
2 cups white vinegar
1 garlic clove, minced
1/2 cup candied or crystallized ginger, diced
2 tablespoons mustard seed

1-1/2 teaspoons chili powder
1 teaspoon ground cloves
1 teaspoon salt
1 cup raisins
1 large onion, chopped

Drain peaches, reserving syrup. Cut peaches into small pieces and set aside. In a heavy medium saucepan, combine peach syrup with remaining ingredients. Boil rapidly uncovered 30 minutes, stirring occasionally. Watch carefully to prevent burning. Stir in peaches. Continue to boil until mixture is thickened, about 30 minutes more. Pour into jars and refrigerate overnight to blend flavors. May be stored in refrigerator for several weeks or frozen.

To serve, thaw overnight in refrigerator. Makes 5 cups.

Curried Seafood Salad

An exotic blend of flavors and textures makes a special company salad.

Condiments such as Toasted Coconut, page 27, toasted slivered almonds, chopped green onions, raisins and Peach Chutney, page 65
Curried Dressing, see below

1 head lettuce
4 stalks celery, chopped
4 green onions, chopped
1/2 lb. cooked medium shrimp
1/2 lb. cooked crabmeat

Curried Dressing:
2 tablespoons Peach Chutney, page 65
1 cup mayonnaise
2 tablespoons tarragon vinegar

2 tablespoons vegetable oil
2 teaspoons curry powder
3 to 4 tablespoons half-and-half

Prepare condiments; set aside. To toast nuts, place on a baking sheet and bake in a 350°F (175°C) oven 10 to 15 minutes, stirring occasionally until lightly browned. Toasted nuts may be stored in freezer. Prepare Curried Dressing; set aside. Tear lettuce into bite-size pieces and place in a salad bowl. Add celery and green onions. Stir in shrimp and crabmeat, reserving some pieces for garnish. Toss with Curried Dressing. Garnish with reserved seafood. Serve condiments in separate bowls. Makes 6 to 8 servings.

Curried Dressing:
Mix all ingredients in a blender or food processor fitted with the metal blade. Taste for seasoning. The curry flavor should just bite or its flavor will be lost in the salad. May be made up to 2 days ahead and refrigerated.

Variation
Substitute 1 pound boneless cooked chicken for the seafood.

After a soup has been refrigerated or frozen, taste for seasoning. Foods lose flavor when they are chilled or frozen.

The large shell-shaped dish holds a superb Curried Seafood Salad. The smaller dishes contain chopped green onions, toasted slivered almonds, Peach Chutney, page 65, and Toasted Coconut, page 27, to garnish the curry.

Party Bombe

The correct pronunciation is bom, *but who cares when it's such a superb dessert!*

1 qt. vanilla ice cream, softened slightly
1/2 cup frozen orange juice concentrate,
   partially thawed
1/3 cup canned crushed pineapple,
   well-drained

1 pint lime sherbet, softened slightly
1 pint orange sherbet, softened slightly
Frosted Flowers, see below, if desired

Place a 6-cup metal, round-bottom bowl or bombe mold in the freezer 10 minutes. Spread vanilla ice cream in bottom and up sides of chilled mold, covering it completely. Freeze until firm. Mix orange juice concentrate and pineapple; spread over vanilla ice cream, coating it well. Do not be concerned if some of the pineapple falls to the bottom. Return mold to freezer to set. Spread an even layer of lime sherbet over pineapple mixture; freeze. Spoon orange sherbet into center. Cover with heavy foil. Freeze until solid. May be frozen several months.

Several hours before serving bombe, dip bottom of mold into warm water to unmold. Turn out onto a chilled plate. Return to freezer immediately to reset. Remove from freezer 10 to 15 minutes before serving. Decorate with Frosted Flowers, if desired. Makes 8 to 10 servings.

Variation
Substitute 1 pint raspberry sherbet for the lime or orange sherbet.

Frosted Flowers

This garnish adds a touch of spring.

Small fresh flowers
1 egg white, unbeaten

2 to 3 tablespoons sugar

Dip flowers into egg white, then into sugar. Let stand several minutes. Dip again into sugar. Refrigerate several hours or until set. Use as garnish on desserts or platters. One egg white is enough to frost 24 small flowers.

Card Party
Velvet Cheese Soup
Salade Niçoise or Chinese Chicken Salad
Frosted Fruit Salad
Crisp Crackers
Lucky Lemon Cake

Velvet Cheese Soup

Savory, golden cheese soup is more than irresistible—it's nourishing too.

1/4 lb. butter or margarine
1/2 cup finely chopped carrots
1/2 cup chopped onion
1/2 cup chopped celery
1/3 cup all-purpose flour
4 cups chicken broth
2 cups milk

3 cups shredded natural Cheddar cheese
  (12 oz.)
1/2 teaspoon Dijon-style mustard
1 teaspoon Worcestershire sauce
6 slices bacon, cooked and crumbled,
  if desired

In a large saucepan, melt butter or margarine. Sauté carrots, onion and celery until soft but not brown, 10 to 15 minutes. Add flour. Cook and stir 2 minutes or until blended. Slowly add 3 cups chicken broth, stirring with a wire whisk until mixture comes to a boil and thickens. Place mixture in a blender or food processor fitted with the metal blade. Blend until smooth. Return mixture to a clean saucepan. Stir in remaining 1 cup broth and milk. Stir in cheese, mustard and Worcestershire sauce. Simmer over low heat until soup is hot and cheese is melted. May be refrigerated up to 2 days or frozen; see freezing table, Soups, page 4.

To serve, reheat soup slowly until hot. Do not boil. Garnish each serving with crumbled bacon, if desired. Makes 8 servings.

Salade Niçoise

Green beans and cucumbers add crunch to a layered main-dish salad.

Vinaigrette, see below
2 boiling potatoes (about 1-1/4 lbs.)
Salted water
3/4 lb. fresh green beans or
    1 (10-oz.) pkg. frozen French-cut green
    beans, cooked
1 head Boston or romaine lettuce

2 (9-1/4 oz.) cans tuna fish, well-drained
Salt and pepper to taste
1 cucumber, thinly sliced
1 (2-oz.) can flat anchovy fillets
1/2 cup pitted ripe olives, halved
3 hard-cooked eggs, cut in wedges
2 tomatoes, cut in wedges

Vinaigrette:
1/4 cup chopped parsley
1 medium garlic clove, crushed
1/4 cup chopped onion
1/4 cup red wine vinegar
2 tablespoons lemon juice
1 teaspoon Dijon-style mustard

1/8 teaspoon sugar
1/2 teaspoon dry basil
1/2 cup olive oil
1/2 cup vegetable oil
Salt and pepper to taste

Prepare Vinaigrette; set aside. Place unpeeled potatoes in a medium saucepan. Cover with salted water. Cook uncovered until barely tender when pierced with a fork. Rinse under cold water to stop cooking. Refrigerate until cold. Peel chilled potatoes and slice by hand or in food processor fitted with the slicing disk; set aside. If using fresh green beans, cut off tips. Place beans in a small amount of salted water. Cover and cook 5 minutes. Beans should still be crisp. Drain and rinse under cold water. Cut to fit horizontally into feed tube of food processor. Slice with slicing disk, julienne style. Line a large salad bowl or deep platter with lettuce leaves. Arrange green beans over lettuce. Drizzle with about 1/4 cup Vinaigrette. Layer tuna fish over green beans. Sprinkle generously with salt, pepper and 1/4 cup Vinaigrette. Cover tuna fish with potato slices. Again sprinkle with salt, pepper and 1/4 cup Vinaigrette. Cover potatoes with overlapping cucumber slices. Pour remaining Vinaigrette over cucumbers. Arrange anchovy fillets lattice-fashion across the top. Place an olive half rounded-side up in the square of each lattice. Cover with plastic wrap and refrigerate at least 1 hour or up to 8 hours.

Before serving salad, alternate wedges of hard-cooked eggs and tomatoes around the edge. Makes 6 to 8 servings.

Vinaigrette:
Mix all ingredients in a blender or food processor fitted with the metal blade. May be refrigerated up to 2 weeks. Makes about 1-1/2 cups.

Variations
Salad may be arranged on individual salad plates.

Two small cooked chicken breasts, sliced, may be substituted for the tuna.

Chinese Chicken Salad

Cut your work in half by buying extra-crisp fried chicken from a take-out restaurant.

1 lb. bacon
5 large fried chicken breasts, cold
1 large head lettuce, shredded
3/4 cup chopped green onions

1 (3-oz.) can chow mein noodles
1 (8-oz.) can water chestnuts,
    drained and sliced
Oriental Dressing, see below

Oriental Dressing:
1/3 cup vegetable oil
1/3 cup soy sauce
1 teaspoon dry mustard

2 tablespoons honey
2 tablespoons ketchup

Cut bacon into 1-inch pieces. Fry until crisp; set aside. Remove bones from chicken. Cut chicken and skin into small strips. In a large bowl, mix bacon pieces and chicken strips with lettuce, onions, noodles and water chestnuts. Refrigerate until chilled or several hours.

Before serving salad, prepare Oriental Dressing. Toss with salad. Makes 8 servings.

Oriental Dressing:
Mix all ingredients in a small bowl. May be stored in refrigerator up to 2 weeks.

How To Make Salade Niçoise

1/After preparing the vegetables, line a salad bowl or platter with lettuce leaves. First place a layer of cooked green beans over the lettuce. Drizzle with about 1/4 cup Vinaigrette. Place a layer of tuna fish over the green beans, sprinkle with salt and pepper and drizzle with 1/4 cup Vinaigrette. Over the tuna fish, place a layer of overlapping potato slices. Again sprinkle with salt and pepper and drizzle with 1/4 cup Vinaigrette.

2/Top the potatoes with sliced cucumbers. Pour remaining Vinaigrette over the cucumbers. Place anchovies on top of the cucumbers in a lattice pattern. Decorate with olive halves. Refrigerate until serving time, then garnish with tomato wedges and hardcooked eggs.

Frosted Fruit Salad

Creamy frosting tops this sparkling gelled salad.

1 (3-oz.) pkg. lime gelatin
1 cup boiling water
1 (7-oz.) bottle 7-Up
1 (8-3/4-oz.) can crushed pineapple
1 banana, peeled and sliced

Pineapple Cream Frosting, see below
Lettuce leaves
1/4 cup shredded sharp Cheddar cheese (1 oz.)
2 tablespoons grated Parmesan cheese

Pineapple Cream Frosting:
1/4 cup sugar
1 tablespoon all-purpose flour
Reserved syrup from pineapple

1 egg, slightly beaten
1/2 cup whipping cream

In a medium bowl, dissolve gelatin in boiling water. Cool. Stir in 7-Up. Refrigerate until partially set. Drain pineapple, reserving syrup. Fold pineapple and banana into gelatin mixture. Pour into an 8-inch square baking dish. Refrigerate until firm. Prepare Pineapple Cream Frosting. Spread frosting over gelatin. Sprinkle with cheese. Cover with plastic wrap. Refrigerate until serving time or up to 2 days.

Before serving, cut salad into rectangles. Serve on a lettuce-lined platter or individual salad plates. Makes 6 to 8 servings.

Pineapple Cream Frosting:

In a small saucepan, combine sugar and flour. Stir in reserved pineapple syrup and egg. Stir over moderate heat until thickened. Remove from heat and cool. In a small bowl, whip cream until stiff. Fold into egg mixture.

To remove excess salt from anchovy fillets, soak them in 3 to 4 tablespoons of milk for 1 hour. Drain and pat dry.

Crisp Crackers

Such a fantastic nutty flavor—no one will believe you made them yourself!

2 cups rolled oats, quick-cooking or regular
1-1/2 cups all-purpose flour
1/3 cup finely ground pecans
1/2 cup shredded coconut
1-1/2 tablespoons brown sugar

1 teaspoon salt
2/3 cup water
1/2 cup vegetable oil
6 tablespoons sesame seeds
Coarse salt or garlic salt

Crush oats with a rolling pin or in a food processor fitted with the metal blade. Place crushed oats, flour, pecans, coconut, brown sugar and 1 teaspoon salt in a large bowl or food processor fitted with the metal blade. Mix until blended. Add water and oil. Blend thoroughly. Preheat oven to 325°F (165°C). Divide dough into 3 balls. Place each ball on a 16" x 12" baking sheet. Roll dough all the way to the edges of the pan. Dough will be very thin. Sprinkle each dough rectangle with 2 tablespoons sesame seeds, then with coarse salt or garlic salt. With a sharp knife or pastry wheel, cut dough into 2-inch squares or diamonds. Bake 30 to 35 minutes or until golden brown. Remove carefully with a spatula. Store in airtight container up to 1 month. May be frozen. Recrisp in a low oven, 250°F (120°C), 5 minutes. Makes 96 crackers.

Lucky Lemon Cake

This delectable frozen cake boasts the texture of cheesecake without the cheese flavor.

2 (3-oz.) pkgs. ladyfingers
2 (14-oz.) cans sweetened condensed milk
8 eggs, separated
2 teaspoons grated lemon peel
14 to 15 tablespoons lemon juice
   (about 6-1/2 oz.)

1/4 teaspoon cream of tartar
Powdered sugar
1 thin slice lemon, if desired

Preheat oven to 375°F (190°C). Lightly grease a 9" x 3" springform pan. Cover bottom of pan with ladyfingers, cutting some to fit. Stand remaining ladyfingers around sides of pan. If necessary, cut bottom ends so tops of ladyfingers are even with top of pan. This prevents tips from getting too brown during baking. In a large bowl, mix condensed milk, egg yolks, lemon peel and lemon juice. In a medium bowl, beat egg whites with cream of tartar until stiff. Fold into lemon mixture. Pour batter into prepared pan. Bake 25 minutes or until top is lightly browned. Cool thoroughly; cover with foil and freeze. Will keep frozen up to 3 months.

Before serving, remove outside ring of springform pan. Dust top of cake with powdered sugar and place a twisted lemon slice in center, if desired. Let stand at room temperature 15 minutes before serving. Leftover cake may be refrozen. Makes 12 servings.

Buffet Suppers

The Spinach-Chicken Soufflé Roll in An Elegant Supper is one of the most spectacular light main dishes you'll ever find. The soufflé is baked in a jelly-roll pan and then rolled around a creamy spinach filling, brimming with mushrooms and chicken. If you have time, make the roll early the day of serving, put it on a baking sheet and leave it at room temperature loosely covered with foil. All you do before serving is heat it in the oven.

You'll find an assortment of dishes which adapt themselves to any holiday or season in the Holiday Open House. Extend greetings to your guests by offering them a glass of Holiday Cranberry Punch, page 154, or Hot Spiced Rum Punch, page 155. Let your table sparkle with a beautiful array of foods. Jeweled Buffet Ham looks and tastes magnificent. Mustard Mousse is a natural with ham but try it with other meat dishes too. For example,

serve it with Barbecued Beef Sandwiches; they're delicious together. You can serve Lemon Snowball proudly. The ingredients are simple, but the end result is delicious and beautiful, guaranteed to bring "oohs" and "ahs" from your guests.

If you want an informal supper menu, the Bowl Game Buffet is ideal. Watching football games on TV is such a popular pastime, why not plan a party around the game? The Bowl Game Buffet is designed to let you sleep late New Year's morning, knowing you have a minimal amount of preparation. Spinach Pom Poms, Liver Pâté Football, Curried Cheese Spread, Barbecued Beef Sandwiches and Glazed Confetti Cake can all be made at least a month in advance and frozen. Spinach Pom Poms don't have to be thawed before baking. If your refrigerator space is limited, leave the Spinach Pom Poms in the freezer and bake them frozen.

An Elegant Supper
Elegant Lazy-Day Soup or Clam Bisque
Lemon Fruit Mold
Cucumbers In Sour Cream Sauce
Spinach-Chicken Soufflé Roll
Royal Mocha Freeze

Elegant Lazy-Day Soup

No one will guess the ingredients.

1 (10-1/2-oz.) can green pea soup
2 (10-1/2-oz.) cans tomato soup
2 (10-1/2-oz.) cans cream of mushroom soup
2 cups milk

3/4 cup water
1-1/4 cups dry sherry
2 (8-oz.) cans crabmeat, drained and diced

In a large saucepan, mix pea soup, tomato soup, mushroom soup, milk, water and sherry. Cook and stir until blended. Do not boil. Stir in crabmeat; heat through. May be refrigerated up to 2 days and reheated. Makes 8 servings.

Clam Bisque

A blushing pink soup with delicate flavor.

6 tablespoons butter or margarine
1 large onion, chopped
6 tablespoons flour
3 (8-oz.) cans minced clams with liquid

2 (8-oz.) bottles clam juice
3 cups half-and-half
3 tablespoons tomato paste
3 tablespoons lemon juice

In a large saucepan, melt butter or margarine. Sauté onion until soft. Stir in flour. Cook and stir until bubbly, about 2 minutes. Slowly stir in clams with liquid and clam juice. Cook and stir until mixture thickens and boils. Cover and simmer 15 minutes. Stir in half-and-half, tomato paste and lemon juice. Heat slowly; do not boil. May be refrigerated overnight or frozen and reheated; see freezing table, Soups, page 4. Makes 10 servings.

Lemon Fruit Mold

To duplicate the photo, double the recipe and use a 13" x 9" glass or porcelain baking dish.

1 (6-oz.) pkg. lemon-flavored gelatin
3 cups boiling water
1/3 cup mayonnaise
1 (3-oz.) pkg. cream cheese, cut in cubes
1/3 cup frozen lemonade concentrate

Fruit for garnish such as sliced strawberries, sliced bananas dipped in lemon juice, drained mandarin oranges, grapes, blueberries, sliced apples dipped in lemon juice, sliced peaches and raspberries

Dissolve gelatin in boiling water. Reserve 3/4 cup gelatin mixture and let stand at room temperature; do not refrigerate at this point or gelatin will harden. Pour remaining gelatin into blender. Add mayonnaise, cream cheese and lemonade concentrate. Blend until smooth. Pour into a 9-inch pie plate or porcelain quiche dish. Refrigerate until firm. Arrange fruits over top of mold in a flower design, as pictured. Or, if desired, arrange fruit in circles, working from the outside in. Refrigerate reserved 3/4 cup gelatin until thick enough to coat a spoon. Carefully spoon thickened gelatin over fruit to glaze. Refrigerate until set or overnight. Makes 8 servings.

Cucumbers In Sour Cream Sauce

A delightful salad to serve with any meal.

3 medium cucumbers
1/2 pint dairy sour cream (1 cup)
1/4 cup chopped green onions
1 teaspoon salt

2 tablespoons white vinegar
3/4 teaspoon sugar
Freshly ground black pepper to taste

Peel cucumbers. Slice into thin rounds. Place slices in a strainer and let drain 1 hour or longer. In a medium bowl, mix remaining ingredients. Add cucumbers and toss lightly. Refrigerate 1 hour before serving or up to 8 hours. Makes 6 to 8 servings.

Spinach-Chicken Soufflé Roll

Spectacular and satisfying, this gourmet treat is worth the extra effort!

4 tablespoons butter or margarine
1/2 cup flour
2 cups milk
1/2 cup grated Parmesan cheese (2 oz.)
1/2 cup shredded Cheddar cheese (2 oz.)

1/4 teaspoon salt
4 egg yolks, slightly beaten
4 egg whites, room temperature
Spinach-Chicken Filling, see below
4 slices Cheddar cheese, cut in triangles

Spinach-Chicken Filling:
2 tablespoons butter or margarine
1/2 cup chopped onion
1/4 lb. mushrooms, chopped
2 (10-oz.) pkgs. frozen chopped spinach,
   thawed and squeezed dry
1 cup diced cooked chicken

1 (3-oz.) pkg. cream cheese
1/3 cup dairy sour cream
2 teaspoons Dijon-style mustard
Dash nutmeg
Salt and pepper to taste

In a medium saucepan over moderate heat, melt butter or margarine. Stir in flour. Cook and stir until blended, about 2 minutes. Slowly add milk, stirring constantly with a whisk. Stir over moderately high heat until batter comes to a boil and thickens. Stir in cheeses and salt. The batter will be very thick. Remove from heat. Add a small amount of batter to egg yolks. Mix well and add egg yolk mixture to saucepan. In a large bowl, beat egg whites until stiff but not dry. Fold a dollop of whites into batter, then gently fold remaining batter into egg whites. Preheat oven to 325°F (165°C). Grease a 15" x 10" x 1" baking sheet or jelly-roll pan. Line with wax paper, leaving a little extra paper at each end; grease and flour wax paper. Pour batter onto prepared wax paper; spread evenly. Bake in lower third of oven 40 to 45 minutes until golden brown and surface springs back when lightly pressed. Prepare Spinach-Chicken Filling; set aside. Remove soufflé from oven; carefully loosen edges of wax paper. Place another piece of wax paper over soufflé. Cover with a tray or another baking sheet and invert. Carefully remove baking sheet now on top and peel off wax paper. Grease another baking sheet; set aside. Spread Spinach-Chicken Filling evenly over top of soufflé. Roll up lengthwise, using the wax paper to help roll. Soufflé may crack. Slide roll seam-side down onto prepared baking sheet. Roll may be refrigerated overnight. It may also be flash frozen or frozen uncovered until solid, then wrapped in freezer foil and returned to freezer.

Before serving, bring soufflé roll to room temperature. If frozen, unwrap and place on a baking sheet to bring to room temperature. Preheat oven to 375°F (190°C). Cover soufflé roll with foil and reheat 20 minutes or until hot. Remove foil. Overlap triangles of cheese down center of roll. Place under broiler until cheese melts and is lightly browned. Slide a spatula under each end of roll and lift onto a platter. Makes 8 servings.

Spinach-Chicken Filling:
In a medium saucepan, melt butter or margarine. Sauté onion and mushrooms until tender. Stir in spinach, chicken, cream cheese and sour cream. Cook and stir until cheese is melted. Add mustard, nutmeg, salt and pepper.

Sautéed Cherry Tomatoes

Bring tomatoes to room temperature before cooking so they will heat up quickly and not fall apart.

2 tablespoons butter or margarine
1/2 cup chopped green onion
2 teaspoons lemon juice
2 lbs. cherry tomatoes,
   washed, stems removed

1/2 teaspoon dry mustard
1/2 teaspoon salt
1/2 teaspoon sugar
1/4 teaspoon freshly ground black pepper
2 tablespoons chopped parsley, if desired

In a medium skillet, melt butter or margarine. Sauté green onion until soft. Add lemon juice, tomatoes, dry mustard, salt, sugar and pepper. Stir constantly over moderately high heat until tomatoes are heated through. Do not overcook or tomatoes will fall apart. Sprinkle with chopped parsley, if desired. Makes 8 servings.

Royal Mocha Freeze

Here's a dainty dish to set before a king.

1 (6-oz.) pkg. chocolate chips (1 cup)
3/4 cup almonds
1 pint whipping cream (2 cups)
1/3 cup brandy

1 (5.5-oz.) can chocolate syrup
1 qt. coffee ice cream, softened
Whipped cream, if desired
Chocolate Leaves, page 7, if desired

In a blender or food processor fitted with the metal blade, coarsely chop chocolate chips and almonds. In a large bowl, mix whipping cream, brandy and chocolate syrup. Beat until thickened but not stiff. Fold in softened ice cream, chopped chocolate chips and almonds. Freeze uncovered until solid on top but still soft inside. Remove from freezer. Stir well to bring chips and almonds up from bottom of bowl. Cover and freeze until solid. May be frozen for several months.

Before serving, spoon frozen mixture into individual serving dishes and garnish with whipped cream and Chocolate Leaves, if desired. Makes 8 to 10 servings.

To freeze leftover tomato paste, line a baking sheet with wax paper. Drop tomato paste by tablespoonfuls onto paper. Freeze until firm. Remove from wax paper and place in plastic bags. Store in freezer and use as needed.

Holiday Open House

Apple-Liver Rumaki
Salmon & Cream Spread
Jeweled Buffet Ham
Noodle Pudding Soufflé
Broccoli With Olive-Nut Sauce
Mustard Mousse
Sunshine Salad
Crunchy Rye Bread
Lemon Snowball

Apple-Liver Rumaki

Apples add a new taste to this longtime favorite.

1/2 cup apple juice
3 tablespoons soy sauce
1 tablespoon honey

1/2 lb. chicken livers
1/2 apple, cut in 24 pieces
1/2 lb. bacon

In a small bowl, mix apple juice, soy sauce and honey. Cut each liver into 2 or 3 pieces. Add liver pieces and apple pieces to apple juice mixture. Marinate covered in refrigerator several hours. Preheat oven to 400°F (205°C). Slice bacon in half crosswise. Wrap a piece of liver and apple in each half slice of bacon. Secure with wooden picks. Place on rack in broiler pan. Brush with marinade. Bake 10 minutes. Place under broiler 5 minutes, turning once or twice until bacon is crisp and livers are cooked. May be frozen and reheated at 400°F (205°C) about 10 minutes; see freezing table, Baked Hors d'Oeuvres, page 4. Makes 24 hors d'oeuvres.

Salmon & Cream Spread

Dill enhances the flavor of this creamy pink spread.

3/4 teaspoon dry dill
3/4 cup dairy sour cream
1 tablespoon prepared white horseradish
1 tablespoon mayonnaise

6 oz. smoked salmon, shredded
1/4 cup chopped green onion
Crackers or bread rounds

In a small bowl, mix dill, sour cream, horseradish and mayonnaise. Stir in salmon and green onion. Refrigerate overnight or up to 2 days. Serve with crackers or bread rounds. Makes 1-1/2 cups.

Jeweled Buffet Ham

Fruit-glazed ham will be the center attraction of your buffet!

1 (8-oz.) can whole-berry cranberry sauce
1 (8-oz.) can jellied cranberry sauce
1 (8-1/4-oz.) can crushed pineapple, drained
1 (11-oz.) can mandarin orange segments,
  drained

1/2 cup orange juice
1 teaspoon seasoned salt
1/2 teaspoon garlic powder
2 to 4 dashes Tabasco sauce
1 (5- to 6-lb.) fully cooked ham

Combine all ingredients except ham in a medium saucepan. Cook over low heat 15 to 20 minutes, stirring occasionally. May be refrigerated several days and reheated. Have butcher slice ham into 1/4-inch slices and tie in original shape. Preheat oven to 350°F (175°C). Place ham in a shallow roasting pan. Bake 1 hour. Remove from oven. Pour off juices. Spoon enough fruit mixture over ham to coat well, mounding fruit generously on the top. Return ham to oven. Bake uncovered 30 minutes; baste occasionally with remaining fruit mixture. Place ham on serving platter. Cut and carefully remove strings. Serve any remaining fruit mixture with ham slices, if desired. Makes 10 to 12 servings.

Noodle Pudding Soufflé

This tasty buffet casserole will become a frequent favorite—company or not.

1 (8-oz.) pkg. medium noodles
Salted water
1/4 lb. butter or margarine, softened
1/2 cup sugar
1/2 pint cottage cheese (1 cup)

1 pint dairy sour cream (2 cups)
1/2 teaspoon salt
2 teaspoons vanilla extract
5 eggs
Cinnamon

Preheat oven to 350°F (175°C). Grease a 13" x 9" baking dish; set aside. In a large saucepan, cook noodles in boiling salted water to cover until tender, 8 to 10 minutes. Drain and set aside. In a large bowl, beat butter or margarine and sugar. Add cottage cheese, sour cream, salt and vanilla. Mix in eggs 1 at a time, beating after each addition. Stir in cooked noodles. Pour into prepared baking dish. Sprinkle top with cinnamon. Bake 50 to 55 minutes, until golden brown. Let stand 5 minutes before cutting into squares. May be frozen and reheated; see freezing table, Casseroles, page 4. Makes 12 servings.

Broccoli With Olive-Nut Sauce

Serve the tasty sauce over cauliflower and asparagus too.

1/4 lb. butter or margarine
1/2 cup slivered almonds (2 oz.)
3 tablespoons lemon juice
1 garlic clove, crushed

1 (2-1/4-oz.) can sliced ripe olives, drained
3 lbs. fresh broccoli, trimmed
Water

Melt butter or margarine in a small skillet. Add almonds, lemon juice, garlic and olives. Let stand 1 hour to blend flavors. Reheat before serving. May be refrigerated overnight and reheated.

Place broccoli in a small amount of boiling water. Cover and cook until tender. Drain. Place in a serving dish. Pour sauce over. Makes 8 servings.

Mustard Mousse

Sweet and tart, this mold brings out the flavor of beef, pork or ham.

1 envelope unflavored gelatin
1/4 cup lemon juice
4 eggs
3/4 cup sugar
3 tablespoons Dijon-style mustard

1/2 teaspoon salt
1/2 cup cider vinegar
1/2 cup water
1/2 pint whipping cream, whipped
2 tablespoons chopped parsley

In a small bowl, sprinkle gelatin over lemon juice and let stand 5 minutes to soften. In a medium saucepan, mix eggs. Add sugar, mustard, salt, vinegar and water. Beat until blended. Add gelatin mixture. Stir constantly over moderate heat until mixture begins to thicken; do not boil. Refrigerate until mixture is thickened and almost set. Oil a 4-cup mold; set aside. Fold whipped cream and parsley into thickened gelatin mixture. Pour into prepared mold. Cover with plastic wrap. Refrigerate several hours or overnight. May be refrigerated up to 3 days.

To unmold, run the tip of a table knife around the edges of mold, dip bottom of mold in warm water and invert onto platter. Makes 8 servings.

How To Make Mustard Mousse

1/In a medium saucepan, add softened gelatin to the egg-mustard mixture. Stir constantly over moderate heat until the mixture begins to thicken. Do not let the mixture boil.

2/After the mixture has thickened in the refrigerator, fold in the whipped cream and chopped parsley. Pour the mixture into an oiled mold and refrigerate to set.

Sunshine Salad

Honey and poppy seeds heighten the flavor.

1 bunch romaine lettuce
2 bunches red leaf lettuce
Sunshine Dressing, see below
1/2 red onion, thinly sliced

2 avocados, peeled and sliced
16 to 20 cherry tomatoes
Salt and pepper to taste

Sunshine Dressing:
1 cup cider vinegar
1 cup vegetable oil

1/2 cup honey
2 teaspoons poppy seeds

Wash lettuce and shake off excess water. Tear into bite-size pieces. Wrap in paper towels, place in plastic bags and refrigerate overnight to crisp. Prepare Sunshine Dressing. Refrigerate until ready to use.

To serve salad, put greens in a very large bowl. Add onion, avocados, tomatoes and dressing. Toss well. Season with salt and pepper. Makes 8 to 10 servings.

Sunshine Dressing:
Mix all ingredients in a small bowl, in a blender or in a tightly covered jar until blended. May be refrigerated up to 1 week. Makes 1-1/4 cups.

Variation

Substitute 1 (8-oz.) can mandarin oranges, drained, and 1 (16-oz.) can grapefruit sections, drained for cherry tomatoes.

Crunchy Rye Bread

If you'd like a change from garlic bread, keep one or two of these tasty loaves in your freezer.

1/3 cup butter or margarine, softened
1/2 teaspoon celery seed
1/4 teaspoon paprika

1/4 teaspoon salt
3/4 cup shredded Swiss cheese (3 oz.)
1 (1-lb.) round loaf rye bread, unsliced

In a small bowl, mix butter or margarine, celery seed, paprika and salt. Stir in cheese. Make 2 lengthwise and 5 crosswise cuts through loaf, leaving bottom crust intact. Spread butter mixture in between cuts and over top and sides of loaf. May be refrigerated or frozen; see freezing table, Breads, page 4.

Before serving bread, bring to room temperature. Preheat oven to 375°F (190°C). Unwrap bread, place on a baking sheet and bake 30 minutes. Bread will slice easier if bottom crust is cut off. Makes 8 servings.

Lemon Snowball

Dazzle your guests with this snow-capped lemon cloud!

2 envelopes unflavored gelatin
4 tablespoons cold water
1 cup boiling water
1 cup granulated sugar
Dash salt
1 (12-oz.) can frozen orange juice concentrate,
  thawed
2 tablespoons lemon juice
Grated peel of 1 lemon

1 pint whipping cream (2 cups)
1 (about 10-oz.) angel-food cake,
  cut in 1-inch cubes
1/2 pint whipping cream (1 cup)
4 tablespoons powdered sugar
1 (4-oz.) pkg. shredded coconut
Green garden leaves such as mint (not holly)
Strawberries

Line a 12-cup bowl with 2 pieces of wax paper, one on top of the other. Let each piece extend over opposite edges of bowl so all edges are covered; paper will be wrinkled. Set bowl aside. In a large bowl, sprinkle gelatin over cold water. Let stand 5 minutes to soften. Add boiling water; stir until gelatin is dissolved. Stir in granulated sugar, salt, orange juice concentrate, lemon juice and peel. Refrigerate 45 minutes to 1 hour, stirring occasionally, until partially set and mixture mounds when dropped from a spoon. In a large bowl, whip 1 pint cream until it forms soft peaks. Fold gelatin mixture into whipped cream. Spoon a small amount of lemon mixture into bottom of prepared bowl. Scatter several pieces of angel-food cake over lemon mixture. Continue alternating cake and lemon mixture until all is used. Cover with plastic wrap and foil. Refrigerate 1 or 2 days before serving. May also be frozen. Thaw in refrigerator overnight.

Before serving, invert bowl on serving platter. Carefully remove bowl and wax paper. In a small bowl, whip 1/2 pint cream and powdered sugar until stiff. Frost top and sides of molded cake with whipped cream. Press coconut into cream. Surround cake with leaves and strawberries. May be refrigerated several hours. Makes 16 servings.

Bowl Game Buffet

Liver Pâté Football
Spinach Pom Poms
Curried Cheese Spread
Barbecued Beef Sandwiches
Overnight Buffet Salad
Copper Penny Carrots
Pineapple-Beet Mold
Glazed Confetti Cake
English Trifle

Liver Pâté Football *Photo on page 89.*

Molded into a football or served in a crock, it's delicious!

1/4 lb. plus 2 tablespoons butter	1/2 teaspoon salt
1/2 cup chopped onion	1/4 teaspoon pepper
1 small tart apple, peeled and chopped	2 whole canned pimientos,
1 lb. chicken livers	cut in very thin strips
2 to 4 tablespoons whipping cream	Bread rounds or crackers

In a medium skillet over moderate heat, melt 3 tablespoons butter. Sauté onion 5 to 7 minutes until soft and lightly browned. Add apple. Cook and stir until apple is soft enough to mash with a spoon. Place onion-apple mixture in a blender or food processor fitted with the metal blade. In the same skillet, melt 3 tablespoons butter. Sauté livers over high heat 3 to 4 minutes, turning until they are browned outside but pink inside. Add livers to onion-apple mixture. Add 2 tablespoons cream. Process until smooth. If mixture is too thick to blend, add more cream. Place pâté mixture in a small bowl and cool completely. Bring remaining butter to room temperature. Stir it into the cooled pâté. Add salt and pepper. Refrigerate until chilled. Shape chilled pâté into a football. Place pimiento strips across top to simulate laces. Football may be refrigerated up to 5 hours. Or spoon pâté into a crock or small bowls. May be refrigerated in a crock or bowl up to 2 days or frozen; see freezing table, Dips & Spreads, page 4.

Before serving pâté, bring to room temperature. Serve with bread rounds or assorted crackers. Makes 3 cups.

Spinach Pom Poms

So easy to make and freeze!

2 (10-oz.) pkgs. frozen chopped spinach
2 cups packaged herb-seasoned stuffing mix, crushed
1 cup grated Parmesan cheese

Dash nutmeg
6 eggs, beaten
3/4 cup butter, softened
Spicy Mustard Sauce, page 123, if desired

Thaw spinach. Drain; squeeze out all excess moisture. Place in a medium bowl and blend in remaining ingredients. Shape into balls the size of walnuts. Refrigerate or freeze; see freezing table, Unbaked Hors d'Oeuvres, page 4.

Before serving, preheat oven to 350°F (175°C). Lightly grease baking sheets. Place chilled or frozen balls on baking sheets. Bake 10 to 15 minutes or until hot. Drain on paper towels. Serve with wooden picks and Spicy Mustard Sauce, if desired. Makes about 65 hors d'oeuvres.

Curried Cheese Spread

A tangy spread—perfect with cocktails.

2 cups shredded sharp Cheddar cheese (1/2 lb.)
1 (4-oz.) can chopped ripe olives, drained
1/2 cup mayonnaise
1 teaspoon curry powder

1/2 cup chopped green onion
1 small garlic clove, minced
Dash salt
Bread rounds or crackers

In a medium bowl or food processor fitted with the metal blade, blend all ingredients except bread rounds or crackers. Pack into jars or crocks. Refrigerate until chilled. May be refrigerated up to 2 weeks or frozen; see freezing table, Dips & Spreads, page 4.

To serve spread, bring to room temperature. Serve with bread rounds or crackers. Makes 2 cups.

Variation

To serve as a hot hors d'oeuvre, spread toast rounds or crackers with cheese spread. Broil until lightly browned and bubbly. Serve hot.

Barbecued Beef Sandwiches

Convenient, economical and delicious!

1 (4- to 5-lb.) beef brisket
Salt and pepper to taste

Best Barbecue Sauce, see below
Assorted sandwich rolls

Best Barbecue Sauce:
3 (8-oz.) cans tomato sauce
1/2 cup water
1/2 cup chopped onion
1 garlic clove, minced
1/4 cup red wine vinegar
3 tablespoons Worcestershire sauce
1/3 cup brown sugar, firmly packed

2 tablespoons honey
2 teaspoons dry mustard
1 teaspoon chili powder
1 teaspoon salt
1 small lemon, thinly sliced
Dash liquid smoke, if desired

Preheat oven to 325°F (165°C). Sprinkle brisket with salt and pepper. Roast in covered roasting pan 3 to 4 hours until tender when pierced with a fork. Cool and refrigerate. Prepare Best Barbecue Sauce; set aside. Cut excess fat from beef. Slice meat into thin slices. Place a layer of meat in the bottom of a large oven-to-table casserole dish. Spread with a layer of Best Barbecue Sauce. Continue layering meat and sauce until all is used. Cover with aluminum foil. May be refrigerated up to 2 days or frozen; see freezing table, Casseroles, page 4.

Before serving sandwiches, bring meat and sauce mixture to room temperature. Preheat oven to 350°F (175°C). Bake 1 hour or until heated through. Serve with assorted sandwich rolls. Makes 10 to 12 servings.

Best Barbecue Sauce:
Mix all ingredients in a medium saucepan. Bring to boil. Lower heat and simmer uncovered 30 minutes, stirring occasionally. May be frozen. Makes 4 cups.

To begin the Bowl Game Buffet, serve the Liver Pâté Football, page 86. Barbecued Beef for sandwiches, above, is in the casserole and Copper Penny Carrots, page 90, are in the round glass dish. Burgundy-Apple Punch, page 154, is at the top left.

Overnight Buffet Salad

An ideal make-ahead and serve-yourself salad.

1 large bunch spinach
1 head red leaf lettuce
1 head butter lettuce
1 (10-oz.) pkg. frozen peas
1/3 cup chopped green onion
4 hard-cooked eggs, grated
1/2 lb. bacon, cooked and crumbled
1 (1.5-oz.) double pkg. Ranch-style
    salad dressing mix

2 cups mayonaise
1/2 pint dairy sour cream (1 cup)
1/2 pint plain yogurt (1 cup)
Tomato wedges
Green pepper, sliced in rings
Sliced ripe olives
Hard-cooked eggs, sliced or cut in wedges

Wash spinach and lettuce. Tear into small pieces, wrap in paper towels and refrigerate several hours or overnight until dry and crisp. In a 13" x 9" baking dish, layer half the spinach, lettuce, peas, onion, grated eggs and bacon; repeat layers. In a small bowl, combine dry salad dressing mix, mayonnaise, sour cream and yogurt. Spread prepared dressing over entire top of salad making sure edges are covered. Cover with plastic wrap and refrigerate overnight.

To serve salad, garnish top with tomatoes, green pepper rings, olives and slices or wedges of hard-cooked eggs. Makes 12 servings.

Copper Penny Carrots   *Photo on page 89.*

Unique, colorful and worth every cent!

2 lbs. carrots
Water
1 medium red onion, sliced
1 (10-oz.) pkg. frozen peas
1 small green pepper, sliced
1 (10-3/4-oz.) can condensed tomato soup
1/2 cup vegetable oil

1 cup sugar
3/4 cup cider vinegar
1 teaspoon prepared mustard
1 teaspoon Worcestershire sauce
1/2 teaspoon salt
1/4 teaspoon pepper

Peel and slice carrots. Place in a medium saucepan with a small amount of water. Cover and cook until crisp-tender, about 5 minutes; do not overcook. Rinse under cold water to stop cooking; drain and cool. Separate onion slices into rings. In a medium bowl, alternate layers of cooked carrots, peas, onion rings and green pepper. In another medium bowl, mix remaining ingredients until smooth. Pour over vegetables. Cover and refrigerate overnight. May be refrigerated up to 2 weeks. Makes 8 servings.

Pineapple-Beet Mold

Don't use fresh or frozen pineapple—only canned pineapple works in gelatin salads.

1 (6-oz.) pkg. lemon gelatin
3 (8-1/4-oz.) cans diced beets
Water
2 tablespoons white vinegar

1 (20-oz.) can crushed pineapple, undrained
1/2 cup chopped pecans
Salad greens

Place gelatin in a large bowl; set aside. Drain beets, reserving juice. Add enough water to juice to make 2 cups liquid. Place in a small saucepan and bring to a boil. Pour over gelatin; cool. Stir in vinegar, beets, undrained pineapple and pecans. Pour into a 6-cup mold and refrigerate several hours or up to 2 days.

Before serving gelatin, line a platter with salad greens. To unmold gelatin, run the tip of a table knife around the edges, dip bottom of mold in warm water and invert onto salad greens. Makes 10 servings.

Glazed Confetti Cake

The topping is poured on the cake in the pan, making a sweet and crunchy bottom crust.

1-1/4 cups sugar
2 cups flour
2 teaspoons baking soda
2 eggs

1 (1-lb. 1-oz.) can fruit cocktail with syrup
1/4 cup brown sugar, firmly packed
1/2 cup chopped walnuts (2-oz.)
Butter Sauce Topping, see below

Butter Sauce Topping:
1 (6-oz.) can evaporated milk
1 cup sugar
1/4 lb. butter

1 teaspoon vanilla extract
1 cup chopped walnuts (4-oz.)
1-1/2 cups shredded coconut

Preheat oven to 350°F (175°C). Grease a 10-inch Bundt pan; set aside. In a large bowl, beat sugar, flour, baking soda, eggs and fruit cocktail with syrup until blended. Pour into prepared pan. Sprinkle with brown sugar and walnuts. Bake 40 to 50 minutes or until top feels firm. Prepare Butter Sauce Topping. Remove cake from oven. Prick top well with skewer or ice pick. Slowly pour Butter Sauce Topping over cake. With hands, press walnuts and coconut in topping firmly onto cake. Let cool 7 minutes. Invert cake onto serving plate. Cool to room temperature. May be frozen; see Freezing Table, Cakes. Makes 16 servings.

Butter Sauce Topping:
In a small saucepan, bring evaporated milk, sugar and butter to a boil. Cool slightly. Stir in vanilla, walnuts and coconut.

English Trifle

Packaged pound cake gives you a head start.

1 cup sugar
1 tablespoon cornstarch
1/2 teaspoon salt
4 cups milk
8 egg yolks
3 teaspoons vanilla extract
3 tablespoons cream sherry

1-1/2 cups whipping cream
1 (10-3/4-oz.) pkg. pound cake, fresh or
   thawed frozen
1/4 cup seedless raspberry preserves
1/2 pint whipping cream, whipped (1 cup)
Berries, if desired
Candied cherries, if desired

In a large saucepan, combine sugar, cornstarch and salt. Gradually add milk, stirring until smooth. Stir constantly over moderate heat until mixture is thickened and comes to a boil. Boil 1 minute; remove from heat. In a medium bowl, slightly beat egg yolks. Add a little of the hot mixture to the yolks to warm them; add egg yolk mixture to saucepan. Stir over medium heat until custard just begins to boil. Remove from heat. Stir in 1 tablespoon sherry. Strain into a large bowl and chill. Whip 1-1/2 cups whipping cream and fold into custard. Cut pound cake lengthwise into 1/2-inch slices. Sprinkle each slice with sherry. Spread slices with preserves. Cut slices into 2-inch squares. Arrange half the cake squares preserve-side up in the bottom of a large glass bowl. Spread half the custard over the cake. Top with remaining cake squares and custard. Cover with plastic wrap and refrigerate overnight or up to 2 days.

Before serving trifle, frost with additional whipped cream. Garnish with berries or candied cherries, if desired. Makes 10 servings.

Freeze extra egg whites in plastic ice cube trays, 1 white per cube. To release frozen cubes, dip bottom of tray in hot water. Store egg white cubes in plastic bags in freezer. Thaw at room temperature as needed.

Dinner Parties

Dinnertime is the most popular time for entertaining. In this section, you'll find three different types of dinner parties: A Candlelight Dinner, the ultimate in gourmet dining, Summer Night Barbecue, for dining on the patio, and the casual and easy Buffet For A Crowd.

A Candlelight Dinner is a meal for your most discriminating guests. Shrimp, marinated overnight in a sweet and tart dressing that's accented with dill, makes a savory hors d'oeuvre. Steak In A Bag is quick and easy, yet it tastes like you've worked for hours. Display the steak on a pretty platter in the same brown bag it cooked in. Slit open the top of the bag at the table in front of your guests so you can enjoy their amazement when they realize how the steak was cooked. Carve the meat at the table or return it to the kitchen for slicing. For a splendid finale, bring out the Chocolate Mousse Cake in a circle of Chocolate Leaves. Part of the mousse is baked into the cake and the other part used as a filling. Dessert Coffee, page 149, with a hint of coffee liqueur, adds the final touch of gracious living to the menu.

The Summer Night Barbecue is elegant enough to serve to VIP guests on a candle-lit patio, yet casual enough to spread out on a picnic table. Shish Kabobs are always popular. The textures and tastes from the various meats and vegetables make a pleasing combination. The marinade for the kabobs adds the right touch of flavor and is also good for marinating skirt and flank steaks. Try the two different French bread toppings. You may never make plain garlic bread again!

Invite your neighborhood in for the Buffet for a Crowd. The menu will adapt to as many as you want. If you're expecting neighbors from more than the immediate neighborhood, add Glazed Cocktail Franks and Toasted Brie Wafers, both on page 128. A pitcher of Blushing Sangria or Sangria Blanca, page 150, provides a delicious economical fruit drink. For dinner, proudly present Fabulous Chunky Chili, full of tender beef, sausage and beans. The sweet taste of the corn in the Corn Bread Casserole will offset the mildly spicy chili.

Blue Ribbon Carrot Cake is a wonderful dessert for a crowd. One cake goes a long way, but be prepared. More than once I've seen ecstatic guests go back for thirds and fourths!

Candlelight Dinner
Dilled Shrimp
Zucchini Soup
Parmesan Crescents
Broiled Tomatoes
Steak In A Bag
French-Style Potatoes
Glazed Carrots & Grapes
Chocolate Mousse Cake
Ribbon Cookies

Zucchini Soup

A delightful opening for an important dinner party.

3 lbs. zucchini	2 (10-3/4-oz.) cans chicken broth
2 teaspoons salt	1/2 cup water
1 teaspoon onion powder	1-1/2 cups half-and-half
1 teaspoon garlic powder	Salt and white pepper to taste
1/8 teaspoon white pepper	Chopped chives

Cut ends off zucchini and slice into 1-inch pieces. Place in a 6-quart saucepan. Add salt, onion powder, garlic powder, white pepper, chicken broth and water. Bring to a boil. Cover and cook over moderate heat until tender, about 10 minutes. Place 1/3 of zucchini slices and broth at a time in a blender or food processor fitted with the metal blade. Blend until smooth. Place in a clean saucepan. Stir in half-and-half. Season to taste with salt and white pepper. Stir over moderate heat until heated through. May be refrigerated overnight or frozen; see freezing table, Soups, page 4.

To serve, reheat slowly; do not boil. Garnish with a sprinkling of chives. Makes 8 servings.

Dilled Shrimp

No matter how much you make, it won't be enough.

1-1/2 cups mayonnaise
1/3 cup lemon juice
1/4 cup sugar
1/2 cup dairy sour cream

1 large red onion, thinly sliced
2 tablespoons dry dill
1/4 teaspoon salt
2 lbs. cooked medium shrimp

In a large bowl, mix mayonnaise, lemon juice, sugar, sour cream, onion, dill and salt. Stir in shrimp. Cover and refrigerate overnight. Stir once. Serve with wooden picks. Makes 8 to 10 servings.

Parmesan Crescents

Serve these flaky cheese pastries as hors d'oeuvres or with soups and salads.

3/4 cup butter or margarine,
   room temperature for mixer, cold and cut
   up for food processor
1 pint small curd cottage cheese (2 cups)

1/8 teaspoon salt
2 cups all-purpose flour
1 cup grated Parmesan cheese

In a medium bowl or food processor fitted with the metal blade, blend butter or margarine, cottage cheese and salt. Add flour; mix until blended. Divide dough into 4 flat balls. Refrigerate until cold enough to roll. Preheat oven to 400°F (205°C). Lightly grease baking sheets; set aside. On a floured sheet of wax paper, roll out 1 ball of dough at a time to a 9- or 10-inch round. Sprinkle each round with 3 tablespoons Parmesan cheese. Cut each round into 8 pie-shaped wedges. Beginning with wide end of each wedge, roll towards point. Place point-side down on prepared baking sheets. Shape into crescents. Sprinkle tops lightly with remaining Parmesan cheese. Bake 20 to 25 minutes or until golden. Immediately loosen from baking sheets and place on racks to cool. May be frozen; see Freezing Table, Breads. Serve warm. Makes 32 crescents.

Variation

To make smaller crescents for hors d'oeuvres, divide dough into 6 balls and roll each into a 7-inch round.

When making pastry dough with the food processor, do not bring butter or margarine to room temperature. Use it cold from the refrigerator, cut into small pieces. Pastry can then be rolled without refrigerating.

Broiled Tomatoes

A colorful addition to any plate.

2 small garlic cloves, crushed
3 tablespoons chopped green onions
1/4 cup butter or margarine, melted
1/2 cup breadcrumbs

2 tablespoons chopped parsley
1 teaspoon dry basil
4 medium tomatoes

In a small bowl, mix all ingredients except tomatoes. Cut tomatoes in half crosswise. Place in an 11" x 9" baking dish and spread with breadcrumb mixture. Refrigerate until ready to serve or up to 5 hours.

To serve, bring to room temperature. Place under broiler until crumbs are lightly browned. Makes 8 servings.

Steak In A Bag

A zesty coating flavors this marvelously juicy steak.

1 cup Egg Breadcrumbs, see below
1 (2- to 3-lb.) top sirloin steak,
    cut 2-1/2-inches thick
4 tablespoons butter or margarine, softened
4 tablespoons vegetable oil

1 teaspoon crushed garlic
2 teaspoons seasoned salt
2-1/2 teaspoons seasoned pepper
1 cup shredded sharp Cheddar cheese (4 oz.)

Egg Breadcrumbs:
3 or 4 slices egg bread

Prepare Egg Breadcrumbs; set aside. Remove excess fat from steak. In a small bowl, mix butter or margaine, oil, garlic, seasoned salt and seasoned pepper until blended. Spread on all sides of steak. Mix breadcrumbs and cheese. Press into butter mixture on steak, coating steak well. Place steak in a brown paper grocery bag. Fold end over and secure with staples or paper clips. At this point, steak may be refrigerated several hours.

Before cooking, bring steak to room temperature. Preheat oven to 375°F (190°C). Place bag on a rimmed baking sheet and bake 30 minutes. For medium-rare steak, increase oven temperature to 425°F (220°C) and bake 15 minutes longer. For medium-well steak, reduce heat to 375°F (190°C) and bake 5 more minutes before removing from oven. Remove steak from bag. Let stand 5 minutes before carving into thin slices. Makes 4 to 6 servings.

Egg Breadcrumbs:
Tear bread, including crusts and ends, into pieces and place in blender or food processor fitted with the metal blade. Process until crumbly. Store extra crumbs in plastic bags in freezer and measure out as needed.

Variation
Two steaks may be baked in the same bag. Double the recipe, but keep baking time the same.

French-Style Potatoes

Baked crisp and golden on the outside, these potatoes are appetizingly moist on the inside.

4 lbs. white rose potatoes
Boiling salted water
3 tablespoons butter or margarine

3 tablespoons vegetable oil
1-1/4 teaspoons salt
2 tablespoons chopped parsley, if desired

Peel potatoes. Slice in half lengthwise. Cut into 1-inch slices to make pieces about 1" x 1" x 1-1/2". Cut a thin strip of potato from corners, so edges are slightly rounded. To keep from discoloring, drop each slice as it is trimmed into a bowl of cold water. Drain. In a large saucepan, cook potatoes in boiling salted water to cover for 5 minutes; drain. At this point, potatoes may be held at room temperature several hours or refrigerated covered overnight.

Before baking, preheat oven to 475°F (245°C). Place butter or margarine and oil in a 13" x 9" baking dish. Heat in oven until melted. Add potatoes and salt. Toss gently to coat thoroughly. Bake 50 minutes to 1 hour, stirring occasionally, until potatoes are golden brown. Place on a platter. Sprinkle with parsley, if desired. Makes 8 servings.

How To Make Steak In A Bag

1/After coating the steak with the butter or margarine mixture, prepare the cheese-breadcrumb mixture and press it into the coated steak, covering it completely. Place the steak in a brown paper bag. Fold the end of the bag over and fasten it with staples or paper clips.

2/After the steak is cooked, remove it from the bag and let it stand on the platter for 5 minutes before slicing.

Glazed Carrots & Grapes

Beautifully glazed, you'll love their taste as well as their appearance.

3 (10-oz.) pkgs. frozen carrots in butter sauce
3 tablespoons brown sugar
3 tablespoons vodka

1-1/2 teaspoons cornstarch
2 teaspoons water
1-1/2 cups seedless green grapes

Cook carrots in cellophane packet according to package directions. Slit cellophane open and pour contents into a medium saucepan. Stir in brown sugar and vodka. In a small bowl, mix cornstarch and water until smooth. Stir into carrots. Bring to a boil, stirring constantly. May be kept covered at room temperature several hours.

Before serving, stir in grapes. Cook until heated through. Makes 8 servings.

Chocolate Mousse Cake

Doubly delicious—part of the mousse bakes into a cake, the other part fills it.

7 oz. semisweet chocolate
1/4 lb. unsalted butter
7 eggs, separated
1 cup sugar

1 teaspoon vanilla extract
1/8 teaspoon cream of tartar
Whipped Cream Frosting, see below
Chocolate Leaves, page 7, if desired

Whipped Cream Frosting:
1/2 pint whipping cream (1 cup)
1/3 cup powdered sugar

1 teaspoon vanilla extract

Preheat oven to 325°F (165°C). In a small saucepan, melt chocolate and butter over low heat. In a large bowl, beat egg yolks and 3/4 cup sugar until very light and fluffy, about 5 minutes. Gradually beat in warm chocolate mixture and vanilla. In another large bowl, beat egg whites with cream of tartar until soft peaks form. Add remaining 1/4 cup sugar 1 tablespoon at a time. Continue beating until stiff. Fold egg whites carefully into chocolate mixture. Pour 3/4 of the batter into an ungreased 9" x 3" springform pan. Cover remaining batter and refrigerate. Bake cake 35 minutes. Prepare Whipped Cream Frosting; set aside. Remove cake from oven and cool. Cake will drop as it cools. Remove outside ring of springform pan. Stir refrigerated batter to soften slightly. Spread on top of cake. Refrigerate until firm. Spread Whipped Cream Frosting over tops and sides. Garnish with Chocolate Leaves, if desired. Refrigerate several hours or overnight. May be frozen; see freezing table, Cakes, page 4. Makes 8 to 10 servings.

Whipped Cream Frosting:
In a small bowl, beat whipping cream until soft peaks form. Add powdered sugar and vanilla. Beat until stiff.

Ribbon Cookies

Rich pastry sandwiches your favorite jam or preserves.

1/2 lb. butter or margarine, room temperature
1 cup sugar
2 egg yolks

2 cups all-purpose flour
1 cup chopped walnuts (4 oz.)
1 cup strawberry or raspberry jam

Preheat oven to 325°F (165°C). In a medium bowl, cream butter or margarine until soft. Gradually add sugar and beat until light and fluffy. Add egg yolks; blend. Gradually stir in flour. Stir in nuts. Press half the batter into the bottom of an ungreased 8-inch square pan. Spread jam over. Cover with remaining batter, spreading as evenly as possible. Bake 1 hour or until golden. Cool and cut into 1-inch squares. Makes 64 cookies.

How To Make Chocolate Mousse Cake

2/Remove remaining mousse batter from the refrigerator and stir it. Spread the batter on top of the cake. Fill the dropped cake center with batter and spread it evenly to the edges. Refrigerate until the mousse is firm. After frosting and garnishing, refrigerate the cake several hours or freeze it.

1/As the baked cake cools, the center will fall. When the cake is cool, remove the outside ring of the springform pan.

Summer Night Barbecue
Spinach Dip
Creamy Apricot Mold
Ready Slaw
Shish Kabobs
Mediterranean Pilaf
Cheese-Topped French Bread
Fudge-Coffee Ice Cream Bars

Spinach Dip

Students in my cooking classes say this is their favorite dip!

1 pint dairy sour cream (2 cups)
1 cup mayonnaise
3/4 (2-3/4-oz.) pkg. dry leek soup mix,
   about 1/2 cup
1 (10-oz.) pkg. frozen chopped spinach,
   well-drained

1/2 cup chopped parsley
1/2 cup chopped green onions
1 teaspoon dry dill
1 teaspoon dry Italian salad dressing mix
Assorted raw vegetable dippers,
   see Vegetable Basket, pages 8 and 9

In a large bowl or food processor fitted with the metal blade, combine all ingredients except raw vegetables until blended. Refrigerate until ready to serve or up to 2 days.

Serve dip with assorted raw vegetables such as the Vegetable Basket. Makes 3-1/2 cups.

Creamy Apricot Mold

So delectable you can serve it for dessert!

1 (3-oz.) pkg. lemon gelatin
1 (12-oz.) can apricot nectar
1 unbeaten egg white
2 tablespoons apricot brandy, if desired

1 (1-lb.) can whole apricots, drained
1/2 cup whipping cream
1 (8-1/4-oz.) can crushed pineapple, drained
1 (1-lb.) can apricot halves, drained

Place gelatin in a medium bowl. In a small saucepan, bring apricot nectar to a boil. Pour over gelatin, stirring to dissolve. Refrigerate until cool. Stir in egg white and brandy, if desired. Refrigerate until thickened and almost set. Remove pits from whole apricots. Place pitted whole apricots and thickened gelatin in a blender or food processor fitted with the metal blade; process until blended. In a large bowl, whip cream until stiff. Fold in gelatin mixture and crushed pineapple. Line the bottom of a 6-cup mold with as many apricot halves as will fit, rounded-side down, overlapping them slightly. Gently pour gelatin mixture over apricot halves. Refrigerate several hours or overnight.

To unmold gelatin, run the tip of a table knife around the edges, dip bottom of mold in warm water and invert onto platter. Makes 10 to 12 servings.

Ready Slaw

A sweet and sour red cole slaw made ahead and stored in your refrigerator.

1 small head red cabbage
1 small onion, chopped
2-1/2 teaspoons salt

1/2 cup vegetable oil
3/4 cup sugar
3/4 cup white vinegar

Shred cabbage. Place in a large heat-resistant bowl with onion and salt. Mix well. In a small saucepan, bring oil, sugar and vinegar to a boil. Pour over cabbage; do not stir. Cool. Cover and refrigerate overnight. May be refrigerated several weeks. Makes 8 to 10 servings.

Shish Kabobs

Eight skewers, three different meats, vegetables and fruit make an extraordinary dish!

Marinade Sauce, see below
1 lb. sirloin steak, cut 1-inch thick
1 lb. boneless leg of lamb, cut 1-inch thick
1 lb. pork tenderloin, cut 1/2-inch thick
1 eggplant

4 apples
1 green pepper, seeded
12 mushrooms
1/2 lb. sliced bacon

Marinade Sauce:
1/2 cup vegetable oil
1/4 cup soy sauce
1/2 cup red wine
1 teaspoon ground ginger
2 small garlic cloves, crushed

1-1/2 teaspoons curry powder
2 tablespoons ketchup
1/4 teaspoon pepper
1/4 teaspoon Tabasco sauce

Prepare Marinade Sauce; set aside. Cut beef, lamb and pork into 1-1/2-inch pieces. Place meat in a shallow dish, keeping each type of meat separate. Pour 3/4 of the Marinade Sauce over meat. Cover and refrigerate 24 hours, stirring once or twice. A few hours before serving, peel and slice eggplant 1/2 inch thick; cut into 1-1/2-inch squares. Peel apples and cut into 6 wedges. Cut green pepper in 1-1/2-inch squares. Place eggplant, apples, green pepper and mushrooms in a medium bowl. Add remaining Marinade Sauce. Marinate 2 to 3 hours at room temperature, stirring occasionally.

To cook kabobs, wrap a half slice of bacon around each piece of lamb. On large skewers, alternate beef, mushrooms, lamb, eggplant, pork, green pepper and apple. Barbecue or broil 5 to 10 minutes on each side. Makes 8 servings.

Marinade Sauce:
Blend all ingredients in a blender or food processor fitted with the metal blade.

Mediterranean Pilaf

Turmeric and curry powder add brilliant golden color and delicate flavor.

3 cups chicken broth
1-1/2 cups uncooked long-grain white rice
4 tablespoons vegetable oil
1/2 cup seedless golden raisins

1/2 teaspoon turmeric
1/2 teaspoon curry powder
1-1/2 tablespoons soy sauce

In a 1-quart saucepan, bring chicken broth to a boil. In a medium saucepan, mix rice, oil, raisins, turmeric, curry powder and soy sauce. Pour in chicken broth. Cover and cook over low heat 20 minutes or until all liquid is absorbed and rice is tender. Makes 8 servings.

Cheese-Topped French Bread, page 104, complements the Shish Kabobs and Mediterranean Pilaf.

Cheese-Topped French Bread *Photo on page 103.*

Two fabulous toppings—the fun is in the sampling to choose your favorite!

1 round loaf French bread
Butter

Parmesan Cheese Topping, see below
Cheddar Cheese Topping, see below

Parmesan Cheese Topping:
1 large garlic clove, crushed
1/2 cup grated Parmesan cheese

2 teaspoons paprika
1 cup mayonnaise

Cheddar Cheese Topping:
2-1/2 cups shredded Cheddar cheese (10 oz.)
3 tablespoons dry sherry

1 teaspoon Dijon-style mustard
1/2 teaspoon Tabasco sauce

Cut bread in half horizontally. Toast both halves cut-side up under broiler until top is golden. Spread with butter. Spread one half with Parmesan Cheese Topping and the other half with Cheddar Cheese Topping. May be refrigerated overnight or frozen; see freezing table, Breads, page 4.

Before serving bread, preheat oven to 450°F (230°C). Place bread on a baking sheet. Bake 20 minutes or until hot and bubbly. Place under broiler to brown top lightly, if desired. Cut each half into 8 wedges. Makes 16 wedges.

Parmesan Cheese Topping:
Mix all ingredients in a small bowl.

Cheddar Cheese Topping:
Mix all ingredients in a small bowl.

Variation
Spread cheese toppings on tomato halves or over cooked vegetables. Place under broiler until golden brown and bubbly.

Fudge-Coffee Ice Cream Bars

If you halve the recipe, use a 9-inch square pan.

2-1/2 cups crushed vanilla wafer crumbs
3 oz. unsweetened chocolate
1/4 lb. butter or margarine
2 cups powdered sugar

4 eggs, separated
1 cup pecan halves or large pieces
1/2 gal. coffee ice cream

Sprinkle 1-3/4 cups crumbs over bottom of a 13" x 9" baking dish. In a medium saucepan over low heat, melt chocolate and butter or margarine. Remove from heat. Stir in powdered sugar. Beat egg yolks; stir into chocolate mixture. Beat egg whites until stiff. Fold into chocolate mixture, blending well. Pour chocolate mixture over crumbs in baking dish. Top with pecans. Freeze until solid. Soften ice cream. Spread ice cream over fudge layer and top with·remaining 3/4 cup crumbs. Cover with foil. Freeze until solid. Will keep frozen up to 6 months.

To serve, cut into 2-1/2" x 2-1/4" bars. Makes 16 to 20 servings.

Buffet For A Crowd
Bacon & Tomato Dip
Fiesta Dip
Fabulous Chunky Chili
Corn Bread Casserole
Marinated Vegetable Salad
Frozen Fruit Mold
Blue Ribbon Carrot Cake

Bacon & Tomato Dip

If you make this a day or two ahead, your pre-party work will be easier.

9 slices bacon
3 small tomatoes, peeled and quartered
3 teaspoons prepared mustard
1 (8-oz.) pkg. cream cheese, quartered

1/4 teaspoon Tabasco sauce
1-1/2 cups blanched almonds (6 oz.)
3 tablespoons chopped green onion
Chips or crackers

Fry bacon until crisp; drain and cool. Place tomatoes, mustard, cream cheese and Tabasco sauce in blender or food processor fitted with the metal blade. Blend until smooth. Add almonds, green onion and cooked bacon. Process just until almonds are chopped. Refrigerate several hours or up to 2 days. Serve with chips or crackers. Makes 3 cups.

Fiesta Dip

Assemble this colorful platter just before serving.

3 recipes Guacamole Spread, page 22
2 cups shredded Cheddar cheese (8 oz.)
1-1/2 cups shredded Monterey Jack cheese (6 oz.)
3 medium tomatoes, chopped

2 (4-oz.) cans chopped ripe olives, drained
Parsley sprigs, if desired
Jalapeño peppers, if desired
Taco chips

As close to serving time as possible, spread Guacamole Spread on a 16-inch round platter. Place Cheddar cheese, Jack cheese, tomatoes and olives in pie-shaped wedges or in 1-inch concentric circles on guacamole. Garnish with parsley sprigs and jalapeño peppers, if desired. Serve with taco chips. Makes 16 servings.

How To Make Fiesta Dip

1/Smooth Guacamole Spread over a large round platter. Decorate with cheeses, tomatoes and olives to make a wedge-shape pattern or concentric circles; see the Molded Avocado Pinwheel, page 113.

2/Garnish with parsley sprigs and jalapeño peppers, if desired. Serve immediately with taco chips.

Fabulous Chunky Chili

This recipe may be cut in half, but you'll love having extra chili in the freezer.

4 tablespoons vegetable oil
2 large onions, chopped
4 large garlic cloves, minced
4 lbs. lean stew beef, cut in small cubes
3 lbs. bulk pork sausage
2 (1-lb. 12-oz.) cans whole tomatoes
2 (6-oz.) cans tomato paste
6 tablespoons chili powder

3 teaspoons cumin
1 tablespoon oregano
2 (1-lb.) cans baked beans
2 teaspoons salt
2 teaspoons sugar
2 tablespoons unsweetened cocoa powder
2 (15-oz.) cans kidney beans, drained
1 (15-oz.) can pinto beans, drained

In a large heavy saucepan, heat oil. Sauté onion and garlic until soft but not brown. Add beef and sausage. Cook until brown; pour off fat. Add liquid from tomatoes. Chop tomatoes and add to meat mixture with tomato paste, chili powder, cumin, oregano, baked beans, salt, sugar and cocoa powder. Simmer partially covered 2 hours, stirring often. If too dry, add a little water as it cooks. Stir in kidney beans and pinto beans. Cook 30 minutes longer or until meat is very tender. May be refrigerated or frozen; see freezing table, Stews, page 4.

Before serving chili, remove any excess fat from top. Reheat on stove or in a 350°F (175°C) oven until hot and bubbly. Makes 16 servings.

Corn Bread Casserole

Just the thing to go with chili!

2 large onions, chopped
6 tablespoons butter or margarine
2 eggs
2 tablespoons milk

2 (17-oz.) cans cream-style corn
1 (1-lb.) pkg. cornmeal muffin mix
1/2 pint dairy sour cream (1 cup)
2 cups shredded sharp Cheddar cheese (8 oz.)

Preheat oven to 425°F (220°C). Butter a 13" x 9" baking dish. In a medium skillet, sauté onion in butter or margarine until golden; set aside. In a medium bowl, mix eggs and milk until blended. Add corn and muffin mix. Mix well. Spread corn bread batter into prepared baking dish. Spoon sautéed onion over top. Spread sour cream over onion. Sprinkle with cheese. Bake 35 minutes or until puffed and golden. Let stand 10 minutes before cutting into squares. May be refrigerated or frozen and reheated; see freezing table, Casseroles, page 4. Makes 16 servings.

Marinated Vegetable Salad

Keep these crisp marinated vegetables in your refrigerator for a tasty low-calorie snack.

Wine Vinegar Dressing, see below
1 large head cauliflower
4 stalks celery
4 large carrots
1/4 lb. fresh green beans

2 green peppers
1-1/2 bunches green onions
2 (4-oz.) cans pitted ripe olives, drained
2 (8-3/4-oz.) cans garbanzo beans, drained

Wine Vinegar Dressing:
1-1/2 cups red wine vinegar
1-1/2 cups water
1/2 cup vegetable oil
2 tablespoons sugar
4 garlic cloves, minced

2 teaspoons dry oregano
1 teaspoon dry basil
1/2 cup chopped parsley
2 teaspoons salt
1/4 teaspoon pepper

Prepare Wine Vinegar Dressing; set aside. Separate cauliflower into small flowerets. Cut celery, carrots and green beans into 1-inch diagonal pieces. Cut green pepper into 1-inch square pieces. Place cauliflower, celery, carrots, green beans and green peppers, in a 6-quart saucepan. Pour Wine Vinegar Dressing over and stir. Cover and simmer over moderate heat 5 to 6 minutes. Cut green onions into 1-inch diagonal pieces. Stir green onions, olives and garbanzo beans into vegetables. Simmer 3 minutes longer. Place in a large bowl. Cool. Cover and refrigerate overnight. May be refrigerated up to 2 weeks. Makes 16 servings.

Wine Vinegar Dressing:
Mix all ingredients in a medium bowl.

Frozen Fruit Mold

So delicious you'll want to serve it all year round!

1 (8-oz.) pkg. cream cheese, softened
4 tablespoons dairy sour cream
1 (30-oz.) can fruit cocktail, drained
1 (13-1/2-oz.) can crushed pineapple, drained
1 (11-oz.) can mandarin orange sections, drained

1 (6-1/4-oz.) pkg. miniature marshmallows
1 cup coarsely chopped walnuts (4 oz.)
1 pint whipping cream (2 cups)
Salad greens

Oil a 12-cup mold or Bundt pan or two 6-cup molds; set aside. In a large bowl, mix cream cheese and sour cream until fluffy. Stir in fruit cocktail, pineapple, oranges, marshmallows and walnuts. In a medium bowl, whip cream until stiff. Fold whipped cream into fruit mixture. Pour into prepared mold. Cover with foil and freeze until solid. May be frozen for several months.

At least 1 hour before serving, unmold by running the tip of a table knife around the edges and dipping bottom of mold in hot water; invert onto platter lined with lettuce leaves. Refrigerate on platter 4 to 6 hours or let stand at room temperature about 1 hour before serving. Mold should be served slightly frozen. Any leftover mold may be refrozen. Makes 16 to 20 servings.

Blue Ribbon Carrot Cake

Freeze now and frost later, or frost and refrigerate for several days.

2 cups all-purpose flour
2 teaspoons baking soda
2 teaspoons cinnamon
1/2 teaspoon salt
3 eggs
3/4 cup vegetable oil
3/4 cup buttermilk
2 cups sugar

2 teaspoons vanilla extract
1 (8-oz.) can crushed pineapple, drained
2 cups grated carrots
3-1/2 oz. shredded coconut
1 cup coarsely chopped walnuts (4 oz.)
Buttermilk Glaze, see below
Cream Cheese Frosting, see below

Buttermilk Glaze:

1 cup sugar
1/2 teaspoon baking soda
1/2 cup buttermilk

1/4 lb. butter or margarine
1 tablespoon corn syrup
1 teaspoon vanilla extract

Cream Cheese Frosting:

1/4 lb. butter or margarine, room temperature
1 (8-oz.) pkg. cream cheese, room temperature
1 teaspoon vanilla extract

2 cups powdered sugar
1 teaspoon orange juice
1 teaspoon grated orange peel

Preheat oven to 350°F (175°C). Generously grease a 13" x 9" baking dish or two 9-inch cake pans; set aside. Sift flour, baking soda, cinnamon and salt together; set aside. In a large bowl, beat eggs. Add oil, buttermilk, sugar and vanilla; mix well. Add flour mixture, pineapple, carrots, coconut and walnuts. Stir well. Pour into prepared baking dish or pans. Bake 55 minutes or until wooden pick inserted in center comes out clean. While cake is baking, prepare Buttermilk Glaze. Remove cake from oven and slowly pour glaze over hot cake. Cool cake in pan until glaze is totally absorbed, about 15 minutes. Turn out of pan, if desired. Cool completely. May be frozen; see freezing table, Cakes, page 4. Prepare Cream Cheese Frosting. Frost cake. Refrigerate until frosting is set. May be refrigerated several days. Serve chilled. Makes 20 to 24 servings.

Buttermilk Glaze:

In a small saucepan, combine sugar, baking soda, buttermilk, butter or margarine and corn syrup. Bring to a boil. Cook 5 minutes, stirring occasionally. Remove from heat and stir in vanilla.

Cream Cheese Frosting:

Cream butter or margarine and cream cheese until fluffy. Add vanilla, powdered sugar, orange juice and orange peel. Mix until smooth.

To peel tomatoes, remove stem with the tip of a knife. Immerse tomatoes in boiling water for 10 to 20 seconds; green tomatoes may take longer. Place in cold water to cool. Peel should slip off easily.

Cocktail Parties

Cocktail parties are the most practical way to entertain large groups, but they are a challenge to put together so that everyone—including yourself—has a good time. Detailed pre-party planning is vital if you want to be free to enjoy your guests.

The easiest arrangement is to set all your food out on a lavish buffet table so your guests can help themselves. Cold hors d'oeuvres are seldom a problem if they sit out for several hours.

Do not put out all your food at once, but replenish the platters often so the food always looks fresh. If you want to include hot hors d'oeuvres, chafing dish specialties such as Clam Fondue Dip or Chafing Dish Steak Bites are the easiest. A sample buffet for 50 people might include:

• 1 recipe Molded Avocado Pinwheel or Blue Cheese Mold

• 2 recipes Shrimp Pâté or 1 recipe Mock Liver Pâté

• 2 recipes Herring Salad Appetizer

• 2 recipes Dill Dip with vegetables

• 72 Cucumber Boats With Caviar or 72 Caviar-Stuffed Eggs

• 4 recipes Clam Fondue Dip

• 5 recipes Chafing Dish Steak Bites or 2 recipes Mexican Meatballs, page 17, or 1-1/2 recipes Glazed Cocktail Franks, page 128.

An attractive arrangement of cheese and fruit gives even the most hard-to-please guests a variety of choices.

As you change the number of guests, add or subtract one dish for every eight to ten people. The more people, the more varied your selection should be. It's better to have a choice of four spreads than to have an excessive amount of two spreads.

I make the Molded Avocado Pinwheel and the Blue Cheese Mold in a flan tin that has an indented bottom. When the dish is unmolded, there is a ridge around the top of the mold that holds the garnishes in place.

A punch bowl filled with a sparkling punch at one end of the table helps keep cost and work to a minimum. If you want a mixed-drink punch, try the Whiskey Sour Bowl, page 151. For a lighter alcoholic beverage, serve either the Burgundy-Apple Punch or Amber Ginger Punch, page 154.

If you wish to pass hot hors d'oeuvres, you'll find this section full of tempting and unusual delicacies and almost all may be prepared several months ahead and frozen. Seafood Tartlets and Taco Tartlets are two of my favorites. They are both made in miniature muffin cups and have identical shapes, but the similarity ends there. Seafood Tartlets are bread cups with a delicately flavored seafood filling. Taco Tartlets are ground beef cups filled with a zesty sour cream filling.

Cold Hors d'Oeuvres

Mock Liver Pâté
Molded Avocado Pinwheel
Shrimp Pâté
Holiday Cheese Log
Bacon-Stuffed Cherry Tomatoes
Cucumber Boats With Caviar
Marinated Stuffed Mushrooms
Blue Cheese Mold
Gazpacho-Seafood Dip
Stuffed Litchi Nuts
Dill Dip
Herring Salad Appetizer
Artichoke Dippers
Caviar-Stuffed Eggs

Mock Liver Pâté

No one will guess you started with packaged liver sausage.

1 envelope unflavored gelatin	2 teaspoons white horseradish
2 tablespoons cold water	2 tablespoons Dijon-style mustard
1 (10-1/2-oz.) can beef consommé	1/8 teaspoon Worcestershire sauce
1 (8-oz.) pkg. cream cheese, softened	1/8 teaspoon curry powder
1 (8-oz.) pkg. braunschweiger liver sausage	Cocktail rye or pumpernickel bread

Oil a 3-1/2-cup mold; set aside. In a small bowl, sprinkle gelatin over cold water. Let stand 5 minutes to soften. In a small saucepan, heat consommé just to a boil. Add softened gelatin and stir until dissolved; set aside. In a medium bowl or food processor fitted with the metal blade, mix cream cheese, liver sausage, horseradish, mustard, Worcestershire sauce and curry powder until smooth. Stir in 2/3 cup of the consommé mixture; set aside. Pour remaining consommé into prepared mold. Refrigerate until firm. Pour cream cheese mixture over gelled consommé. Refrigerate several hours or freeze; see freezing table, Molds, page 4.

Unmold pâté before serving. To unmold, run the tip of a table knife around the edges, dip bottom of mold in warm water and invert onto platter. Surround with slices of cocktail rye or pumpernickel bread. Makes 3-1/2 cups.

Molded Avocado Pinwheel

Delight your guests with this impressive spread.

1 envelope unflavored gelatin
1/4 cup cold water
1 cup mashed avocado (2 to 3 avocados)
1 tablespoon lemon juice
1 (0.6-oz.) pkg. dry Italian salad dressing mix
1 pint dairy sour cream (2 cups)
3 tablespoons chopped parsley
Dash Tabasco sauce

2 or 3 drops green food coloring, if desired
Bread rounds or crackers
Assorted garnishes such as cooked baby shrimp,
  chopped green onions, chopped cucumbers,
  chopped ripe olives, red or black caviar,
  chopped tomatoes or a Tomato Rose,
  page 14

Oil a 9-1/2-inch porcelain quiche dish, glass pie dish or a flan tin with indented bottom; see photos on page 116. In a small saucepan, sprinkle gelatin over cold water. Let stand 5 minutes to soften. Cook over medium heat until mixture just comes to a boil and gelatin is dissolved. In a large bowl or food processor fitted with the metal blade, blend avocado, lemon juice, salad dressing mix, sour cream, parsley and Tabasco sauce. Add dissolved gelatin. Mix thoroughly. Stir in 2 or 3 drops of green food coloring, if desired. Pour mixture into prepared mold. Cover with plastic wrap. Refrigerate until firm. May be refrigerated up to 2 days. Do not freeze.

If using a quiche dish or pie dish, it is not necessary to unmold spread. If using a flan tin, unmold before serving. Run the tip of a table knife around the edges, dip bottom of mold in warm water and invert onto platter. Decorate with 4 or 5 suggested garnishes. Serve with bread rounds.or crackers. Makes 3 cups.

Shrimp Pâté

A delectable spread I created for my food processor classes.

1/3 cup mayonnaise
1 (3-oz.) pkg. cream cheese, cut in cubes
3 tablespoons chopped onion
3/4 lb. cooked small shrimp, well-drained
1 tablespoon white horseradish
1 teaspoon Dijon-style mustard

1 teaspoon dry dill
1/2 teaspoon sugar
1/2 teaspoon salt
1 tablespoon lemon juice
1/4 teaspoon Tabasco sauce
Crackers or bread rounds

In a food processor fitted with the metal blade, combine mayonnaise and cream cheese. Add remaining ingredients and mix until blended. Shape into a ball or spoon into a crock. Refrigerate several hours or overnight for flavors to blend. May be refrigerated up to 2 days. Do not freeze.

Serve pâté with crackers or bread rounds. Makes 2 cups.

Holiday Cheese Log

This fabulous log makes any day a holiday.

2 cups shredded sharp Cheddar cheese (1/2 lb.)
1 (3-oz.) pkg. cream cheese, room temperature
1 tablespoon chopped parsley
1/4 cup onion, finely chopped
1/2 teaspoon salt
1 small garlic clove, minced

1 teaspoon Worcestershire sauce
Dash Tabasco sauce
Blue Cheese Frosting, see below
1/2 cup finely chopped pistachio nuts
Thin strips of pimiento, if desired
Bread rounds or crackers

Blue Cheese Frosting:
2 oz. blue cheese
1 (3-oz.) pkg. cream cheese, room temperature

2 tablespoons whipping cream or
    half-and-half

In a large bowl or food processor fitted with the metal blade, blend Cheddar cheese and cream cheese. Add parsley, onion, salt, garlic, Worcestershire sauce and Tabasco sauce. Mix until blended. Place cheese mixture on a large sheet of wax paper. Shape and roll to form a log about 8-inches long and 2 inches in diameter. Wrap wax paper around log. Close ends of wax paper. Freeze log for 30 minutes or until solid. Prepare Blue Cheese Frosting. Remove log from freezer; remove wax paper. Spread frosting evenly on all sides and ends of log. Place in freezer 5 minutes. Remove log from freezer and roll in pistachio nuts, coating sides and ends. Wrap in plastic wrap. Refrigerate several hours before serving. May be refrigerated several days or wrapped in foil and frozen.

To serve, if log is frozen, thaw in refrigerator overnight. Garnish log with pimiento strips shaped in a bow, if desired. Serve with bread rounds or crackers. Makes 8 to 10 servings.

Blue Cheese Frosting:
In a small bowl or food processor fitted with the metal blade, blend all ingredients until smooth and spreadable.

Bacon-Stuffed Cherry Tomatoes *Photo on page 121.*

They won't roll on the platter if you scoop out the bottoms and stand them stem-side down.

2 lbs. bacon
1/2 cup finely chopped green onions

1/2 cup mayonnaise
24 cherry tomatoes

Dice bacon. Fry until crisp. Drain and cool on paper towels. In a medium bowl, mix bacon, green onions and mayonnaise. Remove stems from tomatoes. Place tomatoes stem-side down on cutting board. Cut a thin slice off tops. With a small spoon, scoop out pulp. Invert tomatoes on paper towels 30 minutes to drain. Fill tomatoes with bacon mixture. Refrigerate several hours or overnight. Makes 24 appetizers.

Cucumber Boats With Caviar *Photo on page 121.*

Classy sailing!

2 medium cucumbers
Salt
1 (8-oz.) pkg. cream cheese, room temperature
3/4 teaspoon onion powder

1/4 teaspoon Tabasco sauce
2 to 3 tablespoons dairy sour cream
2 oz. red caviar
Parsley sprigs, if desired

Halve cucumbers lengthwise; scoop out seeds. Sprinkle insides of cucumber halves with salt. Invert on paper towels to drain for several hours. *Dry very well.* In a medium bowl, mix cream cheese, onion powder, Tabasco sauce and sour cream until blended. Gently stir in 3/4 of the caviar. Spoon or pipe caviar mixture through a pastry tube into the cucumbers, mounding slightly. May be refrigerated up to 5 hours.

Before serving, slice cucumbers crosswise into 3/4-inch slices. Garnish each slice with remaining caviar and tiny sprigs of parsley, if desired. Makes about 24 appetizers.

Marinated Stuffed Mushrooms

Try the filling as a dip with garden fresh vegetables.

24 medium mushrooms
1 (12-oz.) bottle Italian salad dressing

Piquant Filling, see below

Piquant Filling:
1 (1/2-oz.) pkg. green onion dip mix
1/2 pint dairy sour cream (1 cup)
1 hard-cooked egg, grated
2 tablespoons pimiento-stuffed green olives,
   chopped

1/4 teaspoon Tabasco sauce
Parsley sprigs

Clean mushrooms and remove stems. Place mushrooms in an 11" x 7" baking dish. Pour Italian dressing over. Marinate in refrigerator several hours or overnight, stirring occasionally. Prepare Piquant Filling; refrigerate.

Before serving mushrooms, spoon or pipe a small amount of filling into each mushroom cap, mounding slightly. Top each mound with a small sprig of parsley. May be refrigerated up to 5 hours. Makes 24 appetizers.

Piquant Filling:
Mix all ingredients in a small bowl until blended. May be refrigerated overnight.

Blue Cheese Mold

A versatile spiced cheese spread—just as tasty without the garnishes.

2 teaspoons unflavored gelatin
1/4 cup cold water
1 pint dairy sour cream (2 cups)
1 (0.6-oz.) pkg. dry Italian salad dressing mix
1/4 cup crumbled blue cheese
1 pint small curd cottage cheese (2 cups)

Assorted garnishes, such as cooked shrimp,
   chopped green onions, sliced cucumbers,
   chopped ripe olives, red or black caviar,
   chopped tomatoes or a Tomato Rose,
   page 14
Bread rounds or crackers

Oil a 9-1/2-inch porcelain quiche dish, glass pie dish or a flan tin with indented bottom; set aside. In a small saucepan, sprinkle gelatin over cold water. Let stand 5 minutes to soften. Cook over moderate heat until mixture just comes to a boil and gelatin is dissolved. In a blender or food processor fitted with the metal blade, combine dissolved gelatin, sour cream, salad dressing mix, blue cheese and cottage cheese until blended. Pour mixture into prepared mold. Cover with plastic wrap. Refrigerate until firm. May be refrigerated up to 2 days.

If using a quiche dish or pie dish, it is not necessary to unmold spread. If using a flan tin, unmold before serving. Run the tip of a table knife around the edge, dip bottom of mold in warm water and invert onto platter. Decorate top with 4 or 5 suggested garnishes; see Molded Avocado Pinwheel photo, page 113. Serve with bread rounds or crackers. Makes 3 cups.

How To Make Blue Cheese Mold

1/Pour the blue cheese mixture into an oiled mold. Cover with plastic wrap and refrigerate until the mixture is firm.

2/Unmold the spread. Arrange the garnishes in concentric circles around the top; see Molded Avocado Pinwheel, page 113.

Gazpacho-Seafood Dip   *Photo on page 121.*

This unusual dip doubles as a cocktail sauce.

1/4 cup chili sauce
1 cup ketchup
2 garlic cloves, crushed
1 green pepper, chopped
1 onion, chopped
1 cucumber, peeled, seeded and chopped
1 large tomato, peeled, seeded and chopped

2 tablespoons vinegar
2 or 3 drops Tabasco sauce
1 tablespoon olive oil
1 teaspoon Worcestershire sauce
Cooked shrimp, crab or desired seafood
Avocado slices, dipped in lemon juice,
  if desired

In a blender or food processor fitted with the metal blade, combine all ingredients except seafood and avocado. Blend. Refrigerate several hours or overnight. May be refrigerated up to 1 week.

To serve dip, place in a small bowl. Surround with seafood and avocado slices, if desired. Makes 3 cups.

Stuffed Litchi Nuts   *Photo of Stuffed Kumquats on page 121.*

Try the delicious filling in pitted prunes, dates or preserved kumquats.

1 (8-oz.) pkg. cream cheese, softened
1/8 teaspoon salt
1 tablespoon sherry

2 (5-oz.) cans litchi nuts, drained
Parsley sprigs

In a small bowl, blend cream cheese, salt and sherry. Spoon or pipe cream cheese mixture into litchi nuts. Top each with a small sprig of parsley. May be refrigerated up to 5 hours. Makes about 36 appetizers.

Dill Dip

Beau monde seasoning is a spice blend available in most supermarkets.

1/2 pint dairy sour cream (1 cup)
1 cup mayonnaise
1-1/2 teaspoons dill
1-1/2 teaspoons beau monde seasoning

1-1/2 teaspoons dehydrated onion flakes
Artichoke Dippers, page 118, or raw
  vegetables, see Vegetable Basket,
  pages 8 and 9

In a small bowl, mix sour cream, mayonnaise, dill, beau monde seasoning and onion flakes until blended. Refrigerate at least 2 hours or up to 2 days. Serve with Artichoke Dippers or raw vegetables. Makes 2 cups.

Herring Salad Appetizer

A Greek version of Italian antipasto.

1 (6-oz.) jar herring pieces, diced
1/2 cup chopped green pepper
1/2 cup chopped red onion
1/2 cup chopped celery

1 (3-1/4-oz.) can pitted ripe olives, halved
1/2 cup chili sauce
Bread rounds or crackers

In a medium bowl, combine all ingredients except bread rounds or crackers. Refrigerate several hours or up to 2 days. Serve with bread rounds or crackers. Makes 2 cups.

Artichoke Dippers

Artichokes won't discolor or taste metallic if cooked in an enamel or stainless steel pan.

1 large artichoke
1/2 lemon
1 tablespoon olive oil

1/2 teaspoon salt
1/2 teaspoon lemon juice
Desired dip or melted butter

Slice 1 inch off top of artichoke. Cut off stem to make a flat base. Remove tough or discolored leaves from around base. With kitchen scissors, trim remaining thorny tips from leaves. Rub base and all cut portions with half a lemon to prevent discoloring. Pour water 2-inches deep into a medium saucepan. Add olive oil, salt and lemon juice. Bring to a boil. Add artichoke. Cover and boil gently over moderate heat 25 to 45 minutes, depending on artichoke's size. Artichoke is done when base can be pierced easily with a knife. Remove artichoke from water. Dip in cold water and drain upside-down on paper towels. Refrigerate covered for several hours or overnight.

Before serving, gently spread artichoke leaves open. Loosen the purple-edged, pale yellow leaves and fuzzy choke in the center. Remove and discard, using a spoon to scrape out fibrous choke. Fit a small glass dish or cup into center of artichoke. Fill with desired dip or melted butter. To eat, twist leaves off artichoke 1 at a time. Dip the tender fleshy end of leaf into dip or melted butter. Draw between teeth; discard remainder of leaf. Makes 4 appetizer servings.

Caviar-Stuffed Eggs

Eggs-traordinary!

6 hard-cooked eggs
4 tablespoons mayonnaise
2 tablespoons finely chopped onion

Dash salt
1 (1-oz.) jar black caviar

Quarter eggs lengthwise; remove yolks. In a small bowl, mix egg yolks, mayonnaise, onion and salt. Cream until smooth. Fill egg white sections with egg yolk mixture. Spoon a small amount of caviar on top of each section. May be refrigerated covered up to 4 hours. Makes 24 appetizers.

Hot Hors d'Oeuvres

Chafing Dish Steak Bites
Sesame Seed Turnovers
Rarebit Savories
Taco Tartlets
Clam Fondue Dip
Beer Batter Franks with Spicy Mustard Sauce
Crab Canapés
Seafood Tartlets
Pâté-Stuffed Mushrooms
Meat Filling For Filo
Filo Triangles
Triple-Cheese Filling For Filo
Spinach Soufflé Triangles
Toasted Brie Wafers
Glazed Cocktail Franks

Chafing Dish Steak Bites

Perfect for an elegant cocktail party.

1 cup plus 2 tablespoons port wine
1/4 cup olive oil
1 garlic clove, minced
2 teaspoons dry mustard
1 teaspoon Worcestershire sauce

1 (2-lb.) beef sirloin steak,
   cut 1-1/2-inches thick
2 tablespoons ketchup
1 tablespoon sugar

In a 13" x 9" glass baking dish, combine 1 cup wine, olive oil, garlic, mustard and Worcestershire sauce; mix well. Add meat, turning to coat both sides. Cover and marinate at room temperature several hours or in refrigerator overnight; turn meat occasionally.

As close to serving as possible, remove steak from marinade. Pour marinade into a small saucepan; set aside. Broil steak to rare or medium-rare. Do not overcook as meat will continue to cook in chafing dish. Cut steak into 3/4-inch pieces; reserve all juices. Place wooden picks in steak bites. Place in chafing dish. Add drippings and juices from meat to marinade in saucepan. Stir in remaining 2 tablespoons wine, ketchup and sugar. Before serving, bring sauce to a boil, stirring constantly. Pour over steak bites. Keep warm in chafing dish over low flame. Makes 10 to 12 appetizer servings.

Sesame Seed Turnovers

Creamy cheese filling wrapped in a tender flaky crust.

1 (3-oz.) pkg. cream cheese,
   room temperature for mixer,
   cold and cut up for food processor
1/4 lb. butter or margarine,
   room temperature for mixer,
   cold and cut up for food processor

1 cup all-purpose flour
Savory Filling, see below
1 egg white, slightly beaten
Sesame seeds

Savory Filling:

2 eggs
2 cups shredded Muenster cheese (8 oz.)
1 tablespoon grated onion

1/4 teaspoon Tabasco sauce
1/8 teaspoon salt

In a medium bowl or food processor fitted with the metal blade, mix cream cheese, butter or margarine and flour until blended. With hands, form mixture into a flat ball. Wrap in wax paper and refrigerate until cold enough to roll. Prepare Savory Filling; set aside. On a lightly floured surface, roll out cold dough 1/8-inch thick. Using a plain round or fluted cookie cutter, cut out 2-1/2-inch rounds. Reroll scraps of dough and continue to cut rounds until all dough is used. Place a teaspoon of filling on each round. Fold rounds in half over filling. With fingers, press edges together. Seal with tines of fork. Brush the tops with slighly beaten egg white. Place sesame seeds in a small bowl. Dip the top of each turnover into seeds. Unbaked turnovers may be frozen; see freezing table, Unbaked Hors d'Oeuvres, page 4.

Before serving turnovers, preheat oven to 375°F (190°C). Bake turnovers on ungreased baking sheet 20 to 25 minutes or until lightly browned. Makes 36 appetizers.

Savory Filling:
Mix eggs in a small bowl. Stir in remaining ingredients.

Rarebit Savories

Spread on English muffins for instant Welsh rarebit.

1/2 lb. Cheddar cheese, cut in cubes
8 slices bacon, chopped, cooked, drained
1 onion quartered

2 teaspoons mayonnaise
1 teaspoon dry mustard
60 slices bread rounds

In a food processor fitted with the metal blade, combine cheese, bacon, onion, mayonnaise and mustard. Process until blended. May be refrigerated overnight or frozen, if desired.

Before serving, spread mixture on bread rounds. Toast under broiler until brown and puffed. Serve immediately. Makes 60 appetizers.

The tray holds, from the top, Stuffed Kumquats, page 117, Bacon-Stuffed Cherry Tomatoes, page 114, Sesame Seed Turnovers, above, Taco Tartlets, page 122, and Cucumber Boats With Caviar, page 115. The glass bowl contains shrimp in Gazpacho-Seafood Dip, page 117.

Taco Tartlets *Photo on page 121.*

The meat forms the crust and the tortillas are in the filling!

Tortilla Chip Filling, see below

1 lb. lean ground beef

2 tablespoons taco seasoning mix

2 tablespoons ice water

1 cup shredded Cheddar cheese (4 oz.)

Tortilla Chip Filling:

1/2 pint dairy sour cream (1 cup)

2 tablespoons taco sauce

2 oz. chopped ripe olives

3/4 cup coarsely crushed tortilla chips

Preheat oven to 425°F (220°C). Prepare Tortilla Chip Filling; set aside. In a medium bowl, mix beef, taco seasoning mix and ice water with hands. Press into bottom and sides of 1-1/2-inch miniature muffin cups, forming a shell. Place a spoonful of filling into each shell, mounding slightly. Sprinkle Cheddar cheese over tops. Bake 7 to 8 minutes. With the tip of a knife, remove tartlets from pan. Serve immediately or cool and freeze; see freezing table, Baked Hors d'Oeuvres, page 4.

To serve tartlets, reheat in a 375°F (190°C) oven 10 to 15 minutes or until hot. Makes about 30 appetizers.

Tortilla Chip Filling:

Mix all ingredients together in a small bowl.

Variation

For a main-dish pie, substitute a 9-inch pie plate for muffin cups. Bake in a preheated 375°F (190°C) oven 45 minutes. Makes 6 main-dish servings.

Clam Fondue Dip

You'll enjoy the extraordinary taste of this variation of popular fondue.

1 (8-oz.) pkg. cream cheese, cut in cubes

1/2 cup milk

1 small garlic clove, crushed

2/3 cup grated Parmesan cheese

3 (6-1/2-oz.) cans minced clams, drained

2 tablespoons dry white wine

1/2 teaspoon Worcestershire sauce

Crackers, bread cubes or vegetable dippers

In a medium saucepan over low heat, melt cream cheese with milk, stirring until smooth. Stir in garlic, Parmesan cheese, clams, wine and Worcestershire sauce. Cook over low heat 3 minutes. May be refrigerated overnight.

Before serving fondue, reheat over low heat. If fondue is too thick, add a tablespoon more wine or milk. Pour into a chafing dish. Serve warm with crackers, bread cubes or vegetable dippers. Makes 6 to 8 servings.

Beer Batter Franks

Tiny batter-dipped franks on wooden picks are delicious, especially with Spicy Mustard Sauce.

3/4 cup all-purpose flour
1/8 teaspoon salt
1/2 cup flat beer
1 tablespoon vegetable oil

1 egg white
24 cocktail franks
Oil for frying
Spicy Mustard Sauce, see below, if desired

In a small bowl, combine flour and salt. Make a well in center; pour in beer and 1 tablespoon oil. Beat with rotary beater until smooth. Let stand at least 1 hour. In a small bowl, beat egg white until stiff. Stir beer batter and fold in beaten egg white. Pour oil about 1/2-inch deep into a skillet. Heat to 400°F (205°C). Place wooden picks into one end of franks. Dip franks into batter; let excess drip back into bowl. Drop into hot oil and fry until golden, about 1 minute on each side. Drain on paper towels. Serve immediately with Spicy Mustard Sauce, if desired. Makes 24 appetizers.

Spicy Mustard Sauce

A tangy sauce much like the one served in Chinese restaurants.

1/3 to 1/2 cup dry mustard
1/2 cup white vinegar

1/2 cup sugar
1 egg yolk

Combine dry mustard and vinegar in a small bowl. Cover and let stand at room temperature overnight. In a small saucepan, combine mustard-vinegar mixture, sugar and egg yolk. Simmer over low heat until slightly thickened. Cover and store in refrigerator up to 1 month. Serve at room temperature. Makes 1-1/3 cups.

Crab Canapés

Flaky refrigerator rolls, separated into layers and topped with a tasty filling.

1 (6-oz.) pkg. frozen crabmeat,
   thawed and drained, or
   1 (7-1/2-oz.) can crabmeat, drained
1 tablespoon chopped green onion
1 cup shredded Swiss cheese (4 oz.)
1/2 cup mayonnaise

1/4 teaspoon curry powder
1/2 teaspoon salt
1 teaspoon lemon juice
1 (8-oz.) pkg. butterflake refrigerator rolls
1 (8-oz.) can water chestnuts,
   drained and sliced

Preheat oven to 400°F (205°C). Grease a baking sheet; set aside. In a medium bowl, combine crabmeat, green onion, cheese, mayonnaise, curry powder, salt and lemon juice. Mix well. Separate each roll into 3 layers, making 36 pieces. Place pieces on prepared baking sheet. Spoon a small amount of crabmeat mixture on each piece. Top with a slice of water chestnut. Bake 12 minutes or until puffed and brown. Serve hot. May be frozen and reheated; see freezing table, Baked Hors d'Oeuvres, page 4. Makes 36 appetizers.

Seafood Tartlets

Ready-made bread makes delicate pastry shells.

1 loaf thin-sliced sandwich bread
6 tablespoons butter or margarine, melted

Seafood Filling, see below
Paprika

Seafood Filling:
1 cup mayonnaise
1/3 cup grated Parmesan cheese
1/3 cup shredded Swiss cheese
1/3 cup chopped onion

1/4 teaspoon Worcestershire sauce
2 drops Tabasco sauce
2 oz. cooked small baby shrimp
2 oz. cooked crabmeat, flaked

Preheat oven to 400°F (205°C). With a rolling pin, flatten slices of bread. Using a 2-1/2-inch cookie cutter, cut 2 rounds from each slice. Dip each round into melted butter or margarine, coating both sides. Press into 1-1/2-inch miniature muffin cups. Bake 10 minutes or until golden brown. Remove from oven; cool in pans. Prepare Seafood Filling. Fill each tart shell with filling. Sprinkle tops with paprika. Place under broiler until golden and bubbly. Remove from pans. Serve immediately or cool and freeze; see freezing table, Baked Hors d'Oeuvres, page 4.

To serve, reheat in a 450°F (230°C) oven 7 to 10 minutes, until hot. Makes 32 appetizers.

Seafood Filling:

In a medium bowl, combine all ingredients except shrimp and crabmeat. Mix until blended. Carefully stir in shrimp and crabmeat.

Variation

Substitute 1/2 pound chopped cooked mushrooms for the seafood.

Pâté-Stuffed Mushrooms

Leftover pâté goes a long way in these gourmet delicacies.

1 lb. medium mushrooms (about 36)   Pâté Filling, see below
4 tablespoons butter or margarine

Pâté Filling:
Reserved mushroom stems   1/2 cup chopped walnuts (2 oz.)
1 lb. mushrooms   1/2 cup Liver Pâté Football, page 86
4 tablespoons butter or margarine   2 tablespoons dry white wine
1/2 cup chopped onion   Salt and pepper to taste

Clean mushrooms. Twist off stems and reserve for filling. Melt butter or margarine in a large skillet. Add mushrooms, cap-side down. Cover and cook over moderately high heat until soft, about 5 minutes. Place in a 13" x 9" baking dish. Prepare Pâté Filling. Spoon filling into mushroom caps, mounding slightly. May be refrigerated covered up to 2 days. Do not freeze.

Before serving mushrooms, bring to room temperature. Preheat oven to 350°F (175°C). Bake mushrooms 5 to 10 minutes or until heated through. Makes 36 appetizers.

Pâté Filling:

Chop reserved mushroom stems and mushrooms. Place in a tea towel a handful at a time and squeeze out as much moisture as possible. Melt butter or margarine in a medium skillet. Cook mushrooms and onions until most of the liquid has evaporated and onions are still soft. Stir in walnuts; toast lightly. Add Liver Pâté. Stir until melted. Stir in wine, salt and pepper. May be frozen; see freezing table, Dips & Spreads, page 4.

Meat Filling For Filo

Cinnamon and allspice add a Mediterranean flavor.

1 lb. ground beef or lamb   1/2 teaspoon cinnamon
1 onion, chopped   1/2 teaspoon ground allspice
1 large garlic clove, minced   1/8 teaspoon pepper
1/2 teaspoon salt   2 tablespoons chopped parsley

In a medium skillet over moderate heat, brown ground meat until crumbly. Add onion and garlic. Stir over medium heat until onion is limp. Pour off any fat. Stir in salt, cinnamon, allspice and pepper. Cool. Stir in parsley. Use a heaping teaspoon of filling for each filo triangle. Makes enough filling for 48 triangles.

Filo Triangles

Impress your most discriminating guests with these delicacies.

1/2 lb. filo or strudel leaves (about 12 sheets)
1/4 lb. butter, melted

Meat Filling For Filo, page 125 or
Triple-Cheese Filling For Filo, page 127

Lay 1 sheet of filo or strudel leaves on a flat surface. Keep remaining sheets covered with a damp towel to prevent them from drying out. Brush the sheet with melted butter. Fold in half cross-wise. Brush again with melted butter. Cut lengthwise in equal strips about 2-inches wide. Place a small amount of filling in a corner of each strip. Fold corner with filling over, enclosing filling and forming a triangle at the top of the strip. Continue to fold the strip, maintaining triangular shape. Brush top with melted butter. Repeat with remaining filo and filling. Triangles may be refrigerated completely covered overnight or frozen; see freezing table, Unbaked Hors d'Oeuvres, page 4.

Before serving triangles, preheat oven to 400°F (205°C). Lightly butter baking sheets. Place thawed or frozen triangles on baking sheets. Bake 15 to 20 minutes or until golden. Serve immediately. Makes 48 appetizers.

How To Make Filo Triangles

1/After brushing filo sheets with butter and cutting them into equal strips, place a small amount of filling in the corner of each strip. Fold the corner with the filling over to enclose the filling, making a triangle at the top of the strip.

2/Continue to fold the strip, alternating the direction of the triangle.

Triple-Cheese Filling For Filo

Three kinds of cheese makes them three times more delicious!

1 egg
1 cup shredded mozzarella cheese (4 oz.)
1/2 cup ricotta cheese
2 tablespoons grated Parmesan cheese

Dash pepper
Dash salt
1/4 teaspoon onion powder

Beat egg in a small bowl. Add cheeses and seasonings. Mix well. Use one teaspoon filling for each filo triangle. Makes enough filling for 48 triangles.

Spinach Soufflé Triangles

Enhance your table with these lightly flavored hot hors d'oeuvres.

1 (11-oz.) pkg. frozen spinach soufflé
9 sheets filo or strudel leaves
1/4 lb. butter, melted

Powdered sugar
Cinnamon

Thaw spinach soufflé. Lay 1 sheet of filo or strudel leaves on a flat surface. Keep remaining sheets covered with a damp towel to prevent them from drying out. Brush the sheet with melted butter. Fold in half crosswise. Brush again with butter. Cut lengthwise into 4 equal strips about 2-inches wide. Place a scant teaspoon of spinach soufflé in a corner of each strip. Do not overfill as filling will rise as it bakes. Fold the filo over spinach soufflé, enclosing it and forming a triangle at the top of the strip. Continue to fold the strip, maintaining triangular shape. Brush top with melted butter. Repeat with remaining filo and spinach soufflé. Triangles may be refrigerated completely covered overnight or frozen; see freezing table, Unbaked Hors d'Oeuvres, page 4.

Before serving triangles, preheat oven to 400°F (205°C). Lightly butter baking sheets. Place thawed or frozen triangles on baking sheets. Bake 15 to 20 minutes or until golden. Sift powdered sugar over and sprinkle with cinnamon. Makes 36 triangles.

Toasted Brie Wafers

Delicious with cocktails, soups or salads.

1/4 lb. butter or margarine, room temperature for mixer, cold and cut up for food processor	1 cup all-purpose flour
	1/2 teaspoon Tabasco sauce
	1/4 teaspoon seasoned salt
1/2 lb. Brie cheese, rind removed, cut in cubes	1/4 cup sesame seeds

In a medium bowl or food processor fitted with the metal blade, mix butter or margarine and cheese. Add flour, Tabasco sauce and seasoned salt; blend. Divide mixture into 4 parts. Shape each into a log 1 inch in diameter. Wrap in wax paper. Refrigerate overnight or freeze.

Before serving, preheat oven to 400°F (205°C). Slice chilled logs 1/4-inch thick. Place each slice 1 inch apart on ungreased baking sheets. Sprinkle tops with sesame seeds. Bake 8 to 10 minutes or until edges are golden brown. Serve immediately or cool and freeze; see freezing table, Baked Hors d'Oeuvres, page 4. Reheat in a 375°F (190°C) oven 5 to 7 minutes. Serve warm. Makes 60 wafers.

Variation

Substitute 1/2 pound sharp Cheddar cheese for Brie cheese.

Glazed Cocktail Franks

Easy to make—easier to eat!

1 (20-oz.) can pineapple chunks	6 gingersnaps
1 (1-lb.) can sauerkraut	1 tablespoon brown sugar
1 (15-oz.) can tomato sauce	60 cocktail franks
1/4 teaspoon pepper	1 (10-oz.) jar currant jelly
1/4 teaspoon ground ginger	

Drain juice from pineapple into a large saucepan. Set pineapple aside. Add sauerkraut, tomato sauce, pepper, ginger, gingersnaps and brown sugar to pineapple juice. Simmer uncovered 30 minutes, stirring occasionally. Add cocktail franks, currant jelly and reserved pineapple chunks. Cook, stirring occasionally, until jelly is melted. May be refrigerated overnight.

Before serving, reheat slowly. Pour carefully into a chafing dish. Serve with wooden picks. Makes about 20 servings.

Dessert Buffets

Dessert parties are fun because all the goodies can be set out on the buffet table before your guests arrive. This leaves you free to relax and enjoy yourself as if you were a guest at your own party.

Afternoon Tea offers a beautiful array of desserts. The indescribably rich Chocolate Bonbons and Glazed Fruit Tartlets are two of the most impressive pastries you'll find anywhere. Lemon Tea Bread is not only a pleasant addition to a sweet table, it also goes nicely with salads. Try it with Curried Seafood Salad, page 66.

The Sweet Table Reception is designed for a more formal occasion such as an engagement party or anniversary reception. If you bake and serve Chocolate Chip Cheesecake the same day and don't refrigerate it, the chips will be soft and the cake will have an almost marbelized texture. If you refrigerate or freeze the cake, the chips become crunchy. The Waldorf Torte is a moist, melt-in-your-mouth apple cake. With a food processor to chop the raisins, apples and nuts, you can put the cake together in minutes. A picturesque fruit platter such as the Watermelon Whale, pages 10 and 11, enhances a table of sweets. Serve Fluffy Fruit Dressing, a velvety lemon-flavored sauce, with the fruit or as a dip with strawberries. Sparkling beverages such as Strawberry Wine Punch, page 156, or Amber Ginger Punch, page 154, go well with dessert buffets. Be sure to have plenty of coffee and a pot of Spiced Tea, page 149.

Cookies are always popular and what would the holidays be without giving, receiving and sharing them! A Holiday Cookie Exchange is a marvelous informal get-together. You won't have to spend endless hours in the kitchen and the guests go home with a plateful of cookies and new recipes for their cookie file. Here's how a Cookie Exchange works: Ask each guest to bring one platter or basket filled with a favorite cookie for each of the other guests to sample. Be sure to include how many cookies each guest should bring on the invitation. As an acceptance to the party, ask each guest to mail you the recipe for the chosen cookie. Your job is to make enough copies of everybody's recipies, including your own, to go around. As the guests arrive, present each one with a colored folder containing a copy of each recipe. Make an attractive card for each plate of cookies, such as, "Mary Smith's Peanut Butter Jewels" and place the cards beside the appropriate platters. Then everyone will know who brought which cookie and can match the cookies with the recipes. It's a good idea to supply paper plates and plastic wrap for those who want to take some cookies home.

A fun centerpiece for this party is a *cookie tree.* Choose any flat, sturdy cookie, such as the Butter Cookie Cut-Outs. When you bake them, make a hole near the top of each cookie and place a dried pea or bean in each hole. After the cookies are baked and cooled, remove the pea and insert a ribbon through the hole. Hang the cookies from a decorative branch placed on your table or from a miniature Christmas tree. They will last for several weeks, if nobody nibbles on them.

Afternoon Tea
Chocolate Bonbons
Cheesecake Squares
Lemon Tea Bread
Glazed Fruit Tartlets
Sugar & Spice Grapes, page 6
Chocolate Strawberries, page 6

Chocolate Bonbons *Photo on page 145.*

If they love chocolate, they'll swoon over these!

6 oz. semisweet chocolate
5 tablespoons unsalted butter
1/2 cup sugar
2 eggs, slightly beaten
1/2 cup all-purpose flour
1/2 teaspoon baking powder

1 teaspoon vanilla extract
1 cup chopped hazelnuts or almonds (4 oz.)
Velvet Frosting, see below
Garnishes such as halved hazelnuts or almonds,
    halved candied cherries, crystallized
    violets and chocolate sprinkles

Velvet Frosting:
1/2 cup whipping cream
3/4 cup sugar
3 oz. unsweetened chocolate

1 egg yolk, slightly beaten
2 tablespoons butter, softened
1 teaspoon vanilla extract

Preheat oven to 375°F (190°C). Line 1-1/2-inch miniature muffin cups with bonbon papers; set aside. Melt chocolate and butter in the top of a double boiler over hot water. Remove from hot water; stir in sugar. Add eggs, mixing well. Stir in flour, baking powder, vanilla and nuts. Spoon a small amount of chocolate mixture into each prepared muffin cup, filling cups 1/2 to 3/4 full. Bake 8 minutes. Bonbons will be soft and look underbaked but will become firm as they cool. Cool in muffin cups. Prepare Velvet Frosting. Spoon frosting over each bonbon. Garnish tops of bonbons with nuts, candied cherries, crystallized violets or chocolate sprinkles. May be refrigerated up to 1 week or frozen. Serve cold. Makes 55 to 60 bonbons.

Velvet Frosting:
In a small heavy saucepan, mix cream and sugar. Bring to a boil over moderate heat, stirring constantly. Simmer 5 minutes. Add chocolate; stir to melt. Stir a spoonful of chocolate mixture into the egg yolk to warm it slightly. Add egg yolk mixture to saucepan. Add butter; stir until melted. Stir in vanilla.

Cheesecake Squares

Use the other half of the Butter Cookie Dough recipe to make Butter Cookie Cut-Outs, page 142.

1/2 recipe Butter Cookie Dough, page 142   Nut Topping, see below
Cheese Filling, see below

Cheese Filling:

1 (8-oz.) pkg. cream cheese, room temperature   2 tablespoons dairy sour cream
1/4 cup sugar   1 tablespoon lemon juice
1 egg   1/2 teaspoon vanilla extract

Nut Topping:

1/4 cup brown sugar, firmly packed   1/4 teaspoon cinnamon
2 tablespoons flour   1/2 cup chopped nuts (2 oz.)
1 tablespoon butter or margarine

Preheat oven to 350°F (175°C). Press Butter Cookie Dough into bottom of an 8-inch square pan. Bake 25 minutes or until lightly browned. Do not turn off oven. Prepare Cheese Filling and pour over crust. Prepare Nut Topping and sprinkle over filling. Bake at 350°F (175°C) 25 minutes. Cool and cut into 1-1/4-inch squares. May be frozen; see freezing table, Cookies, page 5. Makes 36 squares.

Cheese Filling:
In a medium bowl or food processor fitted with the metal blade, mix cream cheese until smooth. Add remaining ingredients; mix well.

Nut Topping:
With fingers, mix all ingredients in a small bowl until crumbly.

Lemon Tea Bread

Lemony Glaze soaks into the bread, making a rich and moist loaf.

Lemony Glaze, see below
1/3 cup butter, melted
1 cup sugar
3 tablespoons lemon extract
2 eggs
1-1/2 cups all-purpose flour

1 teaspoon baking powder
1 teaspoon salt
1/2 cup milk
1-1/2 tablespoons grated lemon peel
1/2 cup chopped pecans
Butter, if desired

Lemony Glaze:
1/4 cup lemon juice
1/2 cup sugar

Preheat oven to 350°F (175°C). Grease and flour a 9" x 5" loaf pan; set aside. Prepare Lemony Glaze; set aside. In a large bowl, cream butter, sugar and lemon extract until fluffy. Add eggs, beating until mixture is blended. In a medium bowl, sift flour, baking powder and salt. Pour 1/3 of the flour mixture into egg mixture. Add 1/3 of the milk. Stir until blended. Continue adding flour and milk alternately until all is blended. Do not overmix. Fold in lemon peel and pecans. Pour batter into prepared pan. Bake 1 hour or until wooden pick inserted in center comes out clean. Remove bread from oven and immediately pour Lemony Glaze slowly over the top. Let stand 15 to 20 minutes. Turn out onto rack to cool. May be frozen; see freezing table, Breads, page 4.

Before serving bread, bring to room temperature. Cut in thin slices. Serve with butter, if desired. Makes 1 loaf.

Lemony Glaze:
Mix lemon juice and sugar in a small bowl.

Glazed Fruit Tartlets

Sparkling jewels, worthy of your most elegant buffet!

1/4 lb. butter or margarine, softened
1/2 cup sugar
1 egg yolk
1 tablespoon orange juice
1 teaspoon vanilla extract
1 tablespoon grated orange peel
1-3/4 cups all-purpose flour

3 to 4 cups fruits such as sliced bananas, well-drained mandarin orange sections, whole or sliced strawberries, fresh or well-drained canned diced pineapple, seedless grapes and fresh or frozen blueberries
Orange Glaze, see below

Orange Glaze:
1/2 cup sugar
1 tablespoon plus 1-1/2 teaspoons cornstarch
Dash salt

1 cup orange juice
2 teaspoons grated orange peel
1 tablespoon orange-flavored liqueur

Preheat oven to 350°F (175°C). In a medium bowl, beat butter or margarine until fluffy. Do not use a food processor. Gradually mix in sugar, beating until light. Add egg yolk, orange juice, vanilla and orange peel. Mix in flour. Press dough into 2- or 3-inch tartlet molds. Bake 15 to 20 minutes or until lightly browned. Cool in molds 10 minutes. Insert tip of knife between edge of crust and mold and invert crusts 1 at a time into your hand. Cool completely on racks. May be frozen; see freezing table, Baked Pie Crusts, page 5.

Prepare Orange Glaze; set aside. Fill tartlet shells with desired fruit, 1 type of fruit per tartlet. Carefully spoon cooled Orange Glaze over top, covering fruit completely. May be refrigerated up to 8 hours. Makes 24 tartlets.

Orange Glaze:
Mix sugar, cornstarch and salt in a small saucepan. Gradually stir in orange juice until smooth. Heat to boiling, stirring constantly. Boil and stir 2 minutes. Add orange peel. Cover and cool. Stir in orange liqueur.

An assortment of Glazed Fruit Tartlets are shown on the next two pages.

Sweet Table Reception
Lemon-Almond Tartlets
Waldorf Torte
Glazed Chocolate Cake Bars
Watermelon Whale, pages 10 & 11
Fluffy Fruit Dressing
Chocolate Chip Cheesecake

Lemon-Almond Tartlets   Photo on page 145.

Beautiful gems make a treasure chest of your table!

Butter Cookie Dough, page 142
Lemon-Almond Filling, see below
2 cups sliced almonds

1-1/2 cups apricot preserves
Halved strawberries

Lemon-Almond Filling:
3 eggs
3/4 cup sugar
1-1/2 teaspoons grated lemon peel

1/2 cup lemon juice
1/4 teaspoon almond extract
1 cup blanched almonds, finely chopped

Preheat oven to 375°F (190°C). Break off small pieces of Butter Cookie Dough; press into bottom and sides of 2- or 3-inch tartlet molds, making dough as thin as possible. Bake 12 to 15 minutes or until edges are lightly browned. Do not turn off oven. Cool tartlet shells slightly in molds. Prepare Lemon-Almond Filling. Spoon into tartlet shells. Bake at 375°F (190°C) 12 to 15 minutes or until top is firm. Cool 5 minutes in molds. Remove tartlets from molds by pressing tip of a sharp knife into one edge and slipping them out. Cool. May be frozen; see freezing table, Pies, page 4.

Before serving tartlets, sprinkle with sliced almonds. Press preserves through a strainer into a small saucepan. Heat until melted. With a spoon or baster, carefully cover almonds with warm preserves. Garnish each tartlet with half a strawberry. May be stored in a single layer at room temperature overnight. Makes 36 tartlets.

Lemon-Almond Filling:
In a small bowl or food processor fitted with the metal blade, beat eggs until frothy. Blend in remaining ingredients.

Variation
To make 1 large tart, prepare 1/2 recipe Butter Cookie Dough. Press dough into bottom and sides of a 9" x 1" quiche pan with removable bottom. Proceed with recipe.

Waldorf Torte

Raisins, nuts and apples combine in a fabulous fresh apple cake.

1/2 cup all-purpose flour
1 teaspoon baking powder
1 teaspoon salt
1 teaspoon cinnamon
1 cup chopped raisins
2 medium apples, peeled and finely chopped
1 cup chopped walnuts (4 oz.)

4 egg yolks
1 cup sugar
4 egg whites, room temperature
1/4 teaspoon cream of tartar
Whipped Cream Frosting, see below
Walnut halves

Whipped Cream Frosting:
1 cup whipping cream (1/2 pint)
2 tablespoons powdered sugar

Preheat oven to 350°F (175°C). Grease two 9-inch cake pans. Cut 2 circles of wax paper to fit in bottom of each pan. Grease the wax paper; set pans aside. In a medium bowl, sift flour, baking powder, salt and cinnamon. Add raisins, apples and walnuts. Toss well and set aside. In a medium bowl, beat egg yolks and 1/2 cup sugar until very light, thick and fluffy; do not underbeat. Stir yolks into flour-apple mixture. In a large bowl, beat egg whites and cream of tartar until soft peaks form. Gradually add remaining 1/2 cup sugar 1 tablespoon at at time, beating until stiff. Gently fold apple mixture into egg whites. Divide batter between the 2 prepared pans. Bake 35 minutes or until top is set. Cool in pans 15 minutes. Turn out onto rack and remove wax paper. Cool thoroughly. May be frozen; see freezing table, Unfrosted Cakes, page 4.

Several hours before serving torte, prepare Whipped Cream Frosting. Frost between layers, top and sides of torte. Garnish with walnut halves. Refrigerate until serving time. Makes 12 servings.

Whipped Cream Frosting:
In a small bowl, beat cream until soft peaks form. Add powdered sugar and continue to beat until stiff.

Glazed Chocolate Cake Bars

Scrumptious chocolate cake drizzled with ever-so-rich chocolate glaze!

2 cups all-purpose flour
2 cups sugar
1 teaspoon baking soda
1/8 teaspoon salt
1/2 cup unsweetened cocoa powder
1 cup water

1/4 lb. butter or margarine
1/2 cup shortening
2 eggs
1/2 cup buttermilk
1 teaspoon vanilla extract

Chocolate Glaze:
4 oz. unsweetened chocolate
4 tablespoons butter or margarine
4 cups powdered sugar

2 teaspoons vanilla extract
1/3 cup boiling water

Preheat oven to 350°F (175°C). Grease and flour a jelly-roll pan or a 15" x 10" x 1" baking pan; set aside. In a large bowl, sift flour, sugar, baking soda and salt; set aside. In a small saucepan, combine cocoa powder, water, butter or margarine and shortening. Bring to a boil, stirring until butter or margarine and shortening are melted. Pour cocoa mixture over flour mixture. Beat until smooth. Beat in eggs, buttermilk and vanilla. Pour batter into prepared pan. Bake 25 minutes or until wooden pick inserted near center of cake comes out clean. Cool in pan. Prepare Chocolate Glaze. When cake is completely cool, cut into 3" x 2" bars. Place bars on a rack set on a sheet of wax paper. Drizzle with glaze, letting glaze drip down sides of each bar. Refrigerate until firm. May be frozen; see freezing table, Frosted Cakes, page 4. Makes 25 bars.

Chocolate Glaze:
In a medium saucepan over low heat, melt chocolate and butter or margarine. Stir in powdered sugar and vanilla. Add boiling water, stirring until smooth. If glaze does not have a pouring consistency, add up to 2 tablespoons more boiling water a teaspoon at a time.

Fluffy Fruit Dressing

A lemon-flavored topper or dip for fresh fruits and berries.

1/3 cup sugar
1 tablespoon all-purpose flour
1 teaspoon grated lemon peel
1/4 cup lemon juice

1 egg, beaten
1 cup halved marshmallows (2 oz.)
1/2 pint dairy sour cream (1 cup)

In a 1-quart saucepan, combine sugar and flour. Stir in lemon peel, lemon juice and egg, mixing until smooth. Add marshmallows. Stir over low heat until mixture thickens slightly and marshmallows melt, 10 to 15 minutes. Cool slightly. Stir in sour cream. May be refrigerated several days. Makes 2 cups.

How To Make Glazed Chocolate Cake Bars

1/After the cake is baked, use wooden picks as guides for cutting pieces evenly. Insert wooden picks every 2 inches across the short side of the cake and every 3 inches down the long side of the cake.

2/Place the bars on a rack which has a piece of wax paper under it. Drizzle Chocolate Glaze from a spoon over the bars. The glaze should be thin enough to drop from the spoon in fairly even lines. If it is not, add more water 1 teaspoon at a time.

Chocolate Chip Cheesecake

A superb blend of favorite flavors!

Vanilla Wafer Crust, see below
2 (8-oz.) pkgs. cream cheese, softened
3/4 cup sugar
1/2 cup dairy sour cream

1 teaspoon vanilla extract
4 eggs
1 (6-oz.) pkg. chocolate chips

Vanilla Wafer Crust:
1 cup vanilla wafer crumbs
1/4 cup butter or margarine, melted

Sour Cream Topping:
1/2 pint dairy sour cream (1 cup)
1/2 cup sugar

1-1/2 teaspoons lemon juice
1-1/2 teaspoons vanilla extract

Prepare Vanilla Wafer Crust. Preheat oven to 325°F (165°C). In a large bowl, beat cream cheese until fluffy. Gradually add sugar, beating until smooth. Add sour cream, vanilla and eggs. Mix well. Stir in chocolate chips. Pour batter into Vanilla Wafer Crust. Bake 40 minutes or until a 3-inch circle in the center of the cheesecake jiggles when pan is shaken. Cheesecake will become firm as it cools. Remove from oven. Turn heat up to 475°F (245°C). Cool cheesecake in pan 20 minutes. Prepare Sour Cream Topping. Gently spoon topping over cheesecake. Bake 5 minutes only. Cool thoroughly. May be refrigerated up to 4 days or frozen; see freezing table, Cakes, page 4.

Before serving cheesecake, remove outside ring of springform pan and let stand at room temperature 1 hour. Makes 10 servings.

Vanilla Wafer Crust:
Butter a 9" x 3" springform pan. In a small bowl or food processor fitted with the metal blade, mix crumbs and butter or margarine until blended. Press into bottom and 1/2 inch up the sides of prepared pan.

Sour Cream Topping:
Mix all ingredients in a small bowl or food processor fitted with the plastic blade.

Holiday Cookie Exchange
Double-Chocolate Crinkles
Candy Kiss Cookies
Butter Cookie Dough
Butter Cookie Cut-Outs
Holiday Date-Nut Bars
Loving Kisses
Peanut Butter Jewels
Coconut-Date Macaroons
Chewy Nut Bars
Cake Mix Cookies
Chocolate Chip Treats
Choco-Nut Fruit Balls

Double-Chocolate Crinkles   **Photo on page 144**

Freeze them or they'll disappear. And thaw them under wraps so they'll make it to the table!

4 oz. unsweetened chocolate
1/2 cup shortening
2 cups sugar
2 teaspoons vanilla extract
4 eggs

2 cups all-purpose flour
2 teaspoons baking powder
1/2 teaspoon salt
1 (6-oz.) pkg. chocolate chips (1 cup)
1 cup powdered sugar, sifted

Melt chocolate and shortening together in the top of a double boiler over hot but not boiling water. Stir in sugar. Place mixture in a medium bowl; cool. Beat until blended. Add vanilla. Beat in eggs 1 at a time, mixing well after each addition. In another medium bowl, sift flour, baking powder and salt. Stir flour mixture into chocolate mixture. Stir in chocolate chips. Refrigerate dough several hours or overnight.

To bake cookies, preheat oven to 375°F (190°C). Lightly grease baking sheets; set aside. Break off small pieces of chilled dough and form into 1-inch balls. Place powdered sugar in a shallow bowl. Roll cookies in sugar, covering them completely. Place cookies 2 inches apart on prepared baking sheets. Bake 10 minutes. Cookies will be very soft, but will become firm as they cool. Immediately place on racks to cool. May be frozen; see freezing table, Cookies, page 5. Makes about 70 cookies.

Candy Kiss Cookies

One bite reveals the kiss!

Butter Cookie Dough, see below
1 cup finely chopped walnuts or pecans (4 oz.)

60 chocolate candy kisses, unwrapped
Powdered sugar

Preheat oven to 350°F (175°C). Prepare Butter Cookie Dough. Mix nuts into dough. Break off small pieces of dough. Shape piece of dough around candy kiss, making a ball with candy in the center. Repeat with remaining dough and kisses. Place on ungreased baking sheets. Bake 18 to 20 minutes or until cookies are solid and bottoms are lightly browned. Remove from baking sheet and immediately roll in powdered sugar. Cool; roll in sugar again. May be frozen; see freezing table, Cookies, page 5. Makes 60 cookies.

Butter Cookie Dough

To make flaky pastry in your food processor, see page 41.

2-1/2 cups all-purpose flour
1/2 lb. butter or margarine,
    room temperature for mixer,
    cold and cut up for food processor

1/2 cup sugar
1 extra-large egg
1 teaspoon vanilla extract

In a medium bowl or food processor fitted with the metal blade, mix flour and butter or margarine until crumbly. Add sugar, egg and vanilla. Mix until blended. Dough will be slightly dry. Place on a flat surface and knead into a ball. Divide dough into 2 round flat portions. Wrap in wax paper and refrigerate. May be kept in refrigerator up to 1 week. May be frozen; see freezing table, Pastry Dough, page 5.

Use dough as directed in Butter Cookie Cut-Outs, Cheesecake Squares, Candy Kiss Cookies and Lemon-Almond Tartlets.

Butter Cookie Cut-Outs

Use whatever shapes are appropriate for the occasion.

Butter Cookie Dough, see above
Colored sugar

Chocolate sprinkles

Preheat oven to 350°F (175°C). On a lightly floured surface, roll out each portion of Butter Cookie Dough 1/4-inch thick. Cut out desired shapes with cookie cutters. Place on ungreased baking sheets. Sprinkle with colored sugar or chocolate sprinkles. Bake 10 to 15 minutes or until edges turn golden; do not brown. Immediately remove cookies from baking sheets and place on racks; cool. May be frozen; see freezing table, Cookies, page 5. Makes about 60 cookies.

Holiday Date-Nut Bars

A favorite recipe from my holdiay gift classes.

1 (8-oz.) pkg. pitted dates, chopped
1 cup chopped raisins
1 cup chopped walnuts (4 oz.)
1 teaspoon grated orange peel
1-1/2 teaspoons cinnamon
1 cup sugar
1/4 lb. butter or margarine, room temperature

1 teaspoon vanilla extract
2 eggs
2 cups all-purpose flour
2 teaspoons baking powder
1/2 teaspoon salt
2 tablespoons orange juice
Powdered sugar

Preheat oven to 375°F (190°C). Grease 2 baking sheets; set aside. In a large bowl, stir dates, raisins, walnuts, orange peel, cinnamon and 1/2 cup sugar until fruit is coated with sugar; set aside. In a separate bowl, cream butter or margarine, the remaining 1/2 cup sugar and vanilla until light and fluffy. Beat in eggs 1 at a time, mixing well after each addition. Stir in flour, baking powder, salt and orange juice. Add date mixture. Stir until blended. Do not overmix. Dough will be very stiff. Divide dough into 4 portions. Shape 2 logs on each prepared baking sheet. Make logs about 12" x 2" x 1/2". Bake 15 minutes. Although they will be slightly brown, logs will feel very soft and underdone. They will become firm as they cool. Cool 15 minutes. Cut diagonally into 3/4-inch bars. Dust with powdered sugar. May be frozen; see freezing table, Cookies, page 5. Makes 64 bars.

How To Make Holiday Date-Nut Bars

1/After mixing the dough, divide it into 4 equal portions. On a greased baking sheet, shape two portions into 2 narrow logs 12 inches long. Make sure there is enough space between the 2 logs for expansion during baking. Repeat with the remaining 2 portions of dough on another greased baking sheet.

2/Cut each baked and cooled log into eighteen 3/4-inch pieces. Bars will have a more interesting shape if they are cut diagonally. Sprinkle bars with powdered sugar.

Loving Kisses

You'll love the crunch from the grated chocolate and almonds.

3 egg whites, room temperature
1/2 teaspoon salt
1/4 teaspoon cream of tartar
1 cup super-fine granulated sugar
1 teaspoon vanilla extract

1/4 teaspoon almond extract
4 oz. semisweet chocolate, grated
1 cup finely chopped blanched almonds
Cocoa, if desired

Preheat oven to 275°F (135°C). Grease baking sheets; set aside. In a medium bowl, beat egg whites, salt and cream of tartar until soft peaks form. Add sugar 1 tablespoon at a time, beating after each addition. Continue to beat until meringue forms stiff peaks. Mix in vanilla and almond extracts. Carefully fold in grated chocolate and almonds. Drop meringue mixture by half teaspoonfuls onto prepared baking sheets or fit a pastry bag with a notched tip with a 3/8-inch opening and pipe meringue into 1-inch kisses. Bake 20 to 25 minutes or until firm. With a spatula, carefully loosen cookies from baking sheets. Cool on baking sheets. Place cocoa in a small strainer. Using the back of a spoon, sift cocoa lightly over cookies, if desired. May be frozen; see freezing table, Cookies, page 5. Makes about 100 cookies.

Peanut Butter Jewels

Peanut butter and jelly—what could be better?

1/2 cup shortening
1/2 cup peanut butter
1/2 cup granulated sugar
1/2 cup brown sugar, firmly packed
1 egg
2 tablespoons milk

1 teaspoon vanilla extract
1-3/4 cups all-purpose flour
1/2 teaspoon salt
1 teaspoon baking soda
1/3 cup currant jelly

Preheat oven to 375°F (190°C). In a medium bowl, cream shortening and peanut butter. Gradually beat in granulated sugar and brown sugar. Add egg, milk and vanilla. Mix well. In a small bowl, sift flour, salt and baking soda. Gradually add flour mixture to peanut butter mixture, mixing well. Shape dough into 1-inch balls. Place on an ungreased baking sheet. With finger or end of a wooden spoon, press an indentation in the center of each cookie. Bake 8 minutes. Remove from oven. Spoon a dab of jelly into each depressed center, mounding slightly. Return cookies to oven and bake 2 to 5 minutes more or until jelly is set. Place on racks to cool. May be frozen; see freezing table, Cookies, page 5. Makes about 48 cookies.

The glass dish contains, from the top, Double-Chocolate Crinkles, page 141, Chocolate Bonbons, page 130, and Loving Kisses, above. The china platter holds Peanut Butter Jewels, above, and Lemon-Almond Tartlets, page 136.

144

Coconut-Date Macaroons

Marvelous taste in minutes!

1 cup flaked or shredded coconut
1 cup chopped pecans (4 oz.)
1 cup chopped pitted dates

2/3 cup sweetened condensed milk
1 teaspoon vanilla extract

Preheat oven to 350°F (175°C). Generously grease baking sheets; set aside. In a medium bowl, mix all ingredients. Shape into walnut-size balls. Place 1 inch apart on prepared baking sheets. Bake 10 to 12 minutes, until golden brown. May be frozen; see freezing table, Cookies, page 5. Makes about 24 cookies.

Chewy Nut Bars

They'll keep a long time–if you hide them!

3/4 cup all-purpose flour
1/4 teaspoon salt
1/4 teaspoon baking soda
2 cups brown sugar, firmly packed

2 eggs
1 cup chopped walnuts (4 oz.)
Powdered sugar

Preheat oven to 350°F (175°C). Grease a 9-inch square pan or an 11" x 7" baking dish; set aside. Place flour, salt and baking soda in a medium bowl. Add brown sugar and eggs; mix until fluffy. Stir in walnuts. Spread mixture in prepared pan or baking dish. Bake 30 minutes. Cool. Sprinkle with powdered sugar. Cut into 3" x 1" bars. May be frozen; see freezing table, Cookies, page 5. Makes 27 or 22 bars, depending on the size of pan.

Cake Mix Cookies

So easy, youngsters can make them.

1/4 lb. butter or margarine, room temperature
1 (8-oz.) pkg. cream cheese, room temperature
1 egg

1 teaspoon vanilla extract
1 (18.5-oz.) pkg. devil's-food or yellow cake mix
1 (12-oz.) pkg. chocolate chips (2 cups)

Preheat oven to 375°F (190°C). Grease baking sheets; set aside. In a medium bowl, cream butter or margarine and cream cheese. Add egg and vanilla. Gradually stir in cake mix and chocolate chips, mixing thoroughly. Drop by scant teaspoonfuls onto prepared baking sheet. Bake 8 to 10 minutes. Cool 3 to 4 minutes before removing from baking sheet. May be frozen; see freezing table, Cookies, page 5. Makes about 75 cookies.

Chocolate Chip Treats

Cookie monsters won't be able to resist them!

1/2 lb. butter or margarine, room temperature
1-1/2 teaspoons vanilla extract
1 teaspoon salt
1 cup sugar

2 cups all-purpose flour
1 (12-oz.) pkg. chocolate chips (2 cups)
1 cup chopped walnuts or pecans (4 oz.)

Preheat oven to 375°F (190°C). In a medium bowl, blend butter or margarine, vanilla and salt. Gradually beat in sugar. Stir in flour, chocolate chips and nuts. Press evenly in an ungreased 13" x 9" baking pan. Bake 25 to 30 minutes or until golden. Cool completely. Cut into 1-3/4" x 1" bars. May be frozen; see freezing table, Cookies, page 5. Makes 63 bars.

Choco-Nut Fruit Balls

A perfect holiday gift.

1 (8-oz.) pkg. pitted dates
1 cup pitted prunes
1-1/2 cups raisins
2/3 cup chopped semisweet chocolate chips
  or 4 oz. grated semisweet chocolate

1 cup finely chopped nuts (4 oz.)
2 tablespoons rum or brandy
Finely chopped nuts
Powdered sugar
Shredded coconut

In a food processor fitted with the metal blade or in a meat grinder, finely chop dates. Place in a large bowl. Chop prunes and raisins. Add to dates with chocolate chips or grated chocolate, 1 cup finely chopped nuts and rum or brandy. Mix well with hands. Form into small balls. Roll in finely chopped nuts, powdered sugar or shredded coconut. May be stored in airtight containers at room temperature 1 month or frozen; see freezing table, Cookies, page 5. Makes about 70 confections.

Cookies will bake evenly if placed on the middle rack of your oven. If you place one cookie sheet on the middle rack and another on the lower rack, reverse their positions halfway through baking time.

Beverages

Wine punches are popular for large gatherings because they are easy to prepare and economical. They are also flavorful because the blended fruit juices enhance the wine. The white Sangria Blanca and the red Blushing Sangria punches are two of my favorites. Sangria Blanca is lighter in texture and flavor than Blushing Sangria, yet they are both refreshing and can be prepared several days before serving.

It is difficult to estimate how much punch you will need, but figure 2 or 3 drinks per person. For example, Sunshine Punch makes 12 (6-oz.) servings. Therefore, if you plan on serving 2 drinks per person, this recipe will serve 6. Here are a few tips:
- One quart of liquor makes 20 drinks of 1-1/2 ounces each. One fifth of liquor makes 18 drinks of 1-1/2 ounces each.
- One fifth of wine or champagne makes 5 drinks of 5 ounces each. One gallon of wine or champagne makes 26 drinks of 5 ounces each.

- Allow one pound of ice per guest.
- Always place the ice in the glass *before* pouring in the ingredients. This avoids splashing and hastens the chilling process.
- When preparing a punch, all the ingredients should be cold. The ice or ice ring will last longer if the punch is chilled.
- Allow 2 glasses for each person. Many guests will put down an empty glass when they get a fresh drink.
- The number of drinks consumed will depend on the time of day, type of drink, amount of food and season of the year.

In addition to iced drinks, every party needs a soothing hot beverage or two. Coffee is a reliable standby, but for a change, try Spiced Tea at your next luncheon or meeting. The blend of cinnamon, cloves and tea is delightful. Dessert Coffee is unbelievably rich. Serve it in tall, tempered glasses, as you would Irish coffee.

Dessert Coffee

A fabulous ending to a memorable meal.

4 cups hot coffee
1/2 pt. whipping cream (1 cup)
1/2 cup coffee-flavored liqueur

2 tablespoons unsweetened cocoa powder
2 tablespoons sugar
Ground cinnamon, if desired

In a blender container, combine coffee, cream, liqueur, cocoa powder and sugar. Cover and blend 30 seconds. Serve immediately. Sprinkle with cinnamon, if desired. Makes 6 (8-ounce) servings.

Company Hot Chocolate *Photo on page 35.*

For brunch on a cold morning or with cookies later.

2 oz. unsweetened chocolate
2-1/2 cups hot milk
1/3 cup sugar
1/4 teaspoon vanilla extract
1/4 teaspoon salt

1/4 teaspoon cinnamon, if desired
1/4 teaspoon unsweetened cocoa powder,
  if desired
1/2 pint whipping cream, whipped

Break chocolate into pieces and place in blender container. Add hot milk, sugar, vanilla and salt. Cover and blend until chocolate is dissolved. If desired, mix cinnamon and cocoa powder in a small dish. Pour hot chocolate into cups, top with whipped cream and sprinkle with cinnamon-cocoa mixture, if desired. Makes 4 (5-ounce) servings.

Variation

Add 1 tablespoon instant coffee powder with hot milk.

Spiced Tea

If you're expecting a crowd, double or triple the recipe.

1 qt. water
4 tea bags
2 tablespoons lemon juice
2 cinnamon sticks

12 whole cloves
2 teaspoons vanilla extract
2 tablespoons sugar

In a large saucepan, bring water to a boil. Add tea bags, lemon juice, cinnamon sticks, cloves, vanilla and sugar. Let stand 5 minutes. Remove tea bags. Stir until sugar is dissolved. Bring to a boil. Turn off heat, cover and let stand 5 minutes. Strain into a teapot. Serve immediately. Makes 4 (8-ounce) servings.

Sangria Blanca

You'll love the clear version of this popular punch.

1/2 gal. Rhine Garten white wine (64 oz.)
1 cup apple juice
2 tablespoons sugar
2 tablespoons lemon juice
1/4 cup gin

1/4 cup lime juice
1 lemon, sliced
1 orange, sliced
1 (1-pint) box fresh strawberries

In a large pitcher, mix all ingredients except strawberries. Refrigerate at least 24 hours or up to 3 days.

Serve sangria from a pitcher or punch bowl, garnished with strawberries. Or serve in glasses over ice with a strawberry in each glass. Makes 12 (6-ounce) servings.

Blushing Sangria *Photo on page 19.*

Turns an ordinary party into a fiesta!

1 (4/5-qt.) bottle dry red wine
1/4 cup sugar
1 cup orange juice
1 cup pineapple juice

1/2 cup orange-flavored liqueur
1 orange, sliced
1 lemon, sliced
1 apple, sliced

Several days before serving, mix all ingredients in a large pitcher. Refrigerate to blend flavors. May be refrigerated up to 2 weeks.

Serve sangria from a pitcher or punch bowl, or in glasses over ice. Makes 8 (6-ounce) servings.

Margaritas

Here's the authentic way to serve this traditional Mexican cocktail.

1 lime or lemon
Salt
1 cup Tequila
1 (6-oz.) can frozen limeade concentrate

1/4 cup Triple Sec
Juice of 1 lemon
1 egg white
2 cups crushed ice

Cut lime or lemon in half. Rub rims of glasses with cut edge of lime or lemon. Dip rims in salt; set aside. Mix remaining ingredients in blender. Pour into salt-rimmed glasses. Makes 6 (5-ounce) servings.

Fluffy Eggnog

To please everyone, serve incredibly rich eggnog in two bowls—one with liqueur, one without.

12 egg yolks
1-1/4 cups sugar
4 cups milk
12 egg whites

1/2 pt. whipping cream (1 cup)
2 tablespoons vanilla extract
1-1/2 cups Amaretto liqueur
Nutmeg

In a medium bowl, beat egg yolks until thick and smooth. In a medium saucepan, combine beaten egg yolks, 3/4 cup sugar and 3/4 cup milk. Stir constantly over medium-low heat until mixture thickens to a soft custard, 10 to 15 minutes. Cool. In a very large bowl, beat egg whites until frothy. Slowly add remaining 1/2 cup sugar. Beat until soft peaks form. Fold cooled custard into egg whites. In a medium bowl, whip cream until stiff. Add whipped cream, remaining 3-1/4 cups milk and vanilla to custard. Stir gently until blended. Refrigerate several hours or overnight.

Before serving eggnog, stir well. Add liqueur, mixing well. Sprinkle with nutmeg. Makes about 16 (5-ounce) servings.

Special Ramos Fizz

Let your guests enjoy this frothy drink before brunch.

2 oz. gin (1/4 cup)
2 egg whites
1/2 cup whipping cream
2 tablespoons sugar

2 tablespoons lemon juice
1/2 teaspoon vanilla extract
1 cup crushed ice

In a blender container, combine all ingredients. Cover and blend 10 seconds on high speed. Makes 4 (6-ounce) servings.

Whiskey Sour Bowl

How to make delicious and economical cocktails for a crowd.

1 (6-oz.) can frozen orange juice concentrate
1 (6-oz.) can frozen lemonade concentrate
1 tablespoon bitters
2 tablespoons sugar
1 (3/4-qt.) bottle whiskey sour cocktail
    with alcohol

1 (28-oz.) bottle club soda, chilled
1 orange, thinly sliced
1 lemon, thinly sliced
1 (4-oz.) jar maraschino cherries, if desired

In a large pitcher or punch bowl, combine frozen juice concentrates, bitters and sugar. When juices are thawed, stir until blended. Stir in whiskey sour cocktail and club soda. Garnish with orange and lemon slices and cherries, if desired. Makes 18 (4-ounce) servings.

Ice Ring

Keep a second ice ring in your freezer to replace the melted first one.

6 cups water
5 or 6 large green garden leaves
   such as lemon leaves (not holly)
2 lemons, cut in half

1 (1-lb. 1-oz.) can cling peach halves, drained
4 strawberries
2 candied cherries, halved

Fill a 6-cup ring mold half full of water. Freeze until solid. Remove from freezer, place leaves shiny-side up on top of ice. Cut a slice from bottom of lemon halves, so they sit flat. Alternate peach and lemon halves on leaves; tops of fruit should be even and slightly below top of mold. Place a strawberry on each peach half and a cherry half on each lemon half. Carefully pour a small amount of water around fruit and leaves. Return to freezer until frozen. Add more water to fill mold to the top, if necessary. Freeze mold overnight or for several weeks.

The day before serving, unmold ice ring by dipping bottom of mold in cold water; turn out on heavy foil. Wrap ring securely in foil; return to freezer. To serve, unwrap and float ice ring fruit-side up in punch bowl. Makes 1 ice ring.

Gala Champagne Punch

Offer a toast with this sparkling punch!

1 (4/5-qt.) bottle champagne, chilled
1 (4/5-qt.) bottle Chablis wine, chilled
2 (10-oz.) bottles club soda, chilled
4 oz. brandy

3 oz. crème de cassis
Ice or Ice Ring, see above
1 (1-pint) box fresh strawberries

In a large punch bowl, mix champagne, wine, club soda, brandy and crème de cassis. Add ice or Ice Ring. Place a strawberry in each cup. Makes 20 (4-ounce) servings.

If you need the extra room in your refrigerator, chill wine in picnic ice chests packed with ice cubes.

Ice Ring in Gala Champagne Punch.

Holiday Cranberry Punch

To make a more spirited drink, substitute champagne for ginger ale.

2 pints raspberry sherbet
1/2 cup lemon juice
2 cups orange juice

3/4 cup sugar
1-1/2 qts. cranberry juice cocktail (48 oz.)
2 (28-oz.) bottles ginger ale, chilled

Soften 1 pint sherbet. In a punch bowl, combine softened sherbet, lemon juice, orange juice and sugar. Stir to dissolve sugar. Add cranberry juice. Refrigerate up to 5 hours.

Before serving punch, add ginger ale, mixing well. Scoop remaining sherbet into balls and float on top of punch. Makes 30 (4-ounce) servings.

Amber Ginger Punch

White wine and ginger ale blend into a sparkling cool drink.

1 (4/5-qt.) bottle Sauterne wine
1 (28-oz.) bottle ginger ale
1 (6-oz.) can pineapple juice

3 oz. orange-flavored liqueur (1/3 cup)
Lemon slices, if desired
Mint leaves, if desired

In a large pitcher, mix wine, ginger ale, pineapple juice and liqueur. Refrigerate several hours or overnight to blend flavors.

Before serving punch, mix well. Garnish with lemon slices and sprigs of fresh mint, if desired. Makes 12 (4-ounce) servings.

Burgundy-Apple Punch

Frozen cubes of apple juice add flavor as they melt.

2 qts. apple juice
2 (4/5-qt.) bottles Burgundy wine
2 tablespoons lemon juice

1 cup sugar
1 (28-oz.) bottle ginger ale, chilled

Several days before punch is to be served, freeze 1 quart apple juice in ice cube trays. To make punch, combine remaining apple juice, wine, lemon juice and sugar in a punch bowl; blend. Refrigerate until serving time.

Before serving punch, add ginger ale and frozen apple juice cubes. Makes 30 (4-ounce) servings.

Sunshine Punch

Something special for the younger set.

1 (6-oz.) can frozen orange juice concentrate
1 (6-oz.) can frozen lemonade concentrate
1 (6-oz.) can frozen limeade concentrate

4 cups cold water
1 (28-oz.) bottle 7-Up, chilled
Lemon or lime sherbet, if desired

In a large pitcher or punch bowl, combine all ingredients except sherbet. Stir until juices are thawed and blended. Top with scoops of sherbet, if desired. Makes 18 (4-ounce) servings.

Hot Spiced Rum Punch

Spicy warmth for a winter's night.

3 tablespoons whole cloves
3 small oranges
1/2 gallon apple cider

2 cinnamon sticks
1-1/2 cups rum

Preheat oven to 350°F (175°C). Press cloves generously into oranges. Place in a baking dish. Bake 45 minutes. In a large saucepan, heat cider and cinnamon sticks. Prick hot oranges with a fork. Place in a punch bowl or chafing dish. Pour hot cider over oranges. Stir in rum. Serve warm. Makes 12 (6-ounce) servings.

How To Make Hot Spiced Rum Punch

1/Press the pointed end of cloves into oranges. Place in a baking dish and bake 45 minutes.

2/After piercing each hot orange several times with a fork, place the oranges in a punch bowl or chafing dish. Pour hot cider and cinnamon sticks over the oranges, then stir in rum.

Strawberry Wine Punch

A colorful beverage for your holiday buffet or open house.

2 (10-oz.) pkgs. frozen sliced strawberries
   in syrup
1/2 cup sugar
2 (4/5-qt.) bottles rosé wine

1 (6-oz.) can frozen lemonade concentrate
2 cups pineapple juice, chilled
1 (28-oz.) bottle club soda, chilled
Ice or Ice Ring, page 152

In a punch bowl, combine strawberries, sugar and 2 cups rosé wine. Cover and let stand at room temperature 1 hour.

Before serving punch, add frozen lemonade concentrate and pineapple juice. Stir until lemonade is thawed. Stir in remaining wine and club soda. Add ice or Ice Ring. Makes 24 (4-ounce) servings.

Mai Tai Punch

You'll need twenty 4-inch wooden skewers to make this beautiful punch.

1/2 fresh pineapple
20 strawberries
2 (4/5-qt.) bottles Mai Tai mix,
   without alcohol

1 (4/5-qt.) bottle light rum
1 (4/5-qt.) bottle brandy
1 qt. orange juice, chilled
Ice or Ice Ring, page 152

Cut pineapple into thin slices; thread on wooden skewers. Place a strawberry on each skewer. Refrigerate skewers covered overnight, if desired.

In a large punch bowl, mix Mai Tai mix, rum, brandy and orange juice. Add ice or Ice Ring. Place a skewer with fruit in each glass. Fill glasses with punch. Makes 20 (6-ounce) servings.

Island Fruit Punch

A great non-alcoholic punch for a crowd.

1 (16-oz.) bottle Hawaiian Punch concentrate
2-1/2 qts. cold water (10 cups)
2 (46-oz.) cans pineapple juice, chilled

3 qts. orange juice (12 cups), chilled
3 (28-oz.) bottles 7-Up, chilled
Ice or Ice Ring, page 152

In a very large pitcher or punch bowl, mix Hawaiian Punch concentrate and cold water. Stir in pineapple juice, orange juice and 7-Up. Add ice or Ice Ring. Makes 92 (4-ounce) servings.

How Much For How Many

The easiest way to prepare your shopping list for a party or dinner is to follow the recipe ingredient lists, but a number of items you'll want to serve are not prepared from recipes. It's difficult to know how much you'll need of foods such as potato chips, crackers, dips, tossed salad ingredients, vegetable dippers and ice cream. This table will make it easier for you to decide how much of these non-recipe foods to buy.

	FOR 12 SERVINGS	FOR 24 SERVINGS	FOR 48 SERVINGS
APPETIZERS			
Dips, spreads and pâtés	1-1/2 cups	3 cups	5 cups
Nuts	3/4 lb.	1-1/2 lbs.	3 lbs.
Potato chips	2 (6-oz.) pkgs.	4 (6-oz.) pkgs.	8 (6-oz.) pkgs.
Corn chips	2 (9-1/4-oz.) pkgs.	4 (9-1/4-oz.) pkgs.	8 (9-1/4-oz.) pkgs.
Crackers	1/2 lb.	1 lb.	2 lbs.
Bread rounds	2 (8-oz.) pkgs.	4 (8-oz.) pkgs.	8 (8-oz.) pkgs.
MAKE YOUR OWN SUNDAES			
Ice cream (1 large scoop per person)	2 qts.	1 gal.	2 gals.
Fudge or butterscotch sauce (1 oz. per serving)	12 oz.	24 oz.	48 oz.
Strawberry, pineapple or marshmallow sauce (1-1/2 oz. per serving)	18 oz.	36 oz.	72 oz.
Whipping cream, whipped (2 tablespoons per serving)	1/2 pint	1 pint	2 pints
Chopped nuts (2 teaspoons per serving)	1/2 cup	1 cup	2 cups
TOSSED SALAD OR SALAD BAR			
Iceburg or romaine lettuce	2 heads (about 2 lbs.)	4 heads (about 4 lbs.)	8 heads (about 8 lbs.)
Boston or red leaf lettuce	4 heads (about 3 lbs.)	8 heads (about 6 lbs.)	16 heads (about 12 lbs.)
Cherry tomatoes	About 1 lb.	About 2 lbs.	About 4 lbs.
Croutons	1-1/4 cups	2-1/2 cups	5 cups
Cucumbers, sliced	2 med. (about 1-1/2 lbs.)	4 med. (about 3 lbs.)	8 med. (about 6 lbs.)
Green onions, diced	1/2 lb.	1 lb.	2 lbs.
Radishes, sliced	4 to 5 (about 1/4 lb.)	1 bunch (about 1/2 lb.)	2 bunches (about 1 lb.)
Mushrooms, sliced	1/4 lb.	1/2 lb.	1 lb.
Bacon, cooked, crumbled	1 lb.	2 lbs.	4 lbs.
Hard-cooked eggs	3	5	10
Salad dressing			
For tossed salad (1 oz. per serving)	1-1/2 cups (12 oz.)	3 cups (24 oz.)	6 cups (48 oz.)
For salad bar (2 oz. per serving)	3 cups (24 oz.)	6 cups (48 oz.)	12 cups (3 qts.)
FRESH FRUIT FOR PLATTER, WATERMELON BASKET OR WHALE			
Watermelon	1 small (about 6 lbs.)	1 large (about 12 lbs.)	2 large (about 20 lbs.)
Strawberries	1-1/2 (1-pint) baskets	3 (1-pint) baskets	6 (1-pint) baskets
Pineapple	1 small	1-1/2 medium	3 medium
Cantaloupe	1 medium	2 medium	3 medium
Honeydew or casaba melon	1 medium	2 medium	3 medium
Grapes	1 lb.	2 lbs.	4 lbs.
VEGETABLES FOR RELISH TRAYS OR BASKET			
Carrots	1-1/2 lbs.	3 lbs.	6 lbs.
Celery	1-1/2 lbs.	3 lbs.	6 lbs.
Radishes	1 bunch (about 1/2 lb.)	2 bunches (about 1 lb.)	4 bunches (1-1/2 to 2 lbs.)
Cauliflower	1 medium head (about 1-1/2 lbs.	2 medium heads (about 3 lbs.)	3 large heads (about 6 lbs.)
Cherry tomatoes	About 1 lb.	About 2 lbs.	About 4 lbs.
Cucumber or zucchini	2 med. (about 1-1/2 lbs.)	4 med. (about 3 lbs.)	8 med. (about 6 lbs.)
Mushrooms	1 lb.	2 lbs.	4 lbs.
Green beans	1-1/2 lbs.	3 lbs.	6 lbs.
MISCELLANEOUS			
Butter for spreading (1 pat per serving)	1/4 lb.	1/2 lb.	1 lb.
Cream for coffee	1 cup	2 cups	4 cups
Sugar, granulated	1/4 lb.	1/2 lb.	1 lb.
Lemons, sliced for tea	2	4	8
Cookies (3 per serving)	3 doz.	6 doz.	12 doz.
After dinner mints	1/4 lb.	1/2 lb.	1 lb.

CONVERSION TO METRIC MEASURE

ENGLISH		METRIC	FAHRENHEIT (F)	CELSIUS (C)
1/4 teaspoon	=	1.25 milliliters	175°	80°
1/2 teaspoon	=	2.5 milliliters	200°	95°
3/4 teaspoon	=	3.75 milliliters	225°	105°
1 teaspoon	=	5 milliliters	250°	120°
1 tablespoon	=	15 milliliters	275°	135°
1 fluid ounce	=	30 milliliters	300°	150°
1/4 cup	=	0.06 liter	325°	165°
1/2 cup	=	0.12 liter	350°	175°
3/4 cup	=	0.18 liter	375°	190°
1 cup	=	0.24 liter	400°	205°
1 pint	=	0.48 liter	425°	220°
1 quart	=	0.95 liter	450°	230°
1 ounce weight	=	28 grams	475°	245°
1 pound	=	0.45 kilograms	500°	260°

Index

A
A Candlelight Dinner 93-99
A Special Occasion 49, 64-48
An Elegant Supper 74-79
Afternoon Tea 129-135
Amber Ginger Punch 154
Appetizers, see Hors d'Oeuvres,
   Dips & Spreads, Salads,
   Sandwiches and Soups
Apple Puffed Pancake 34
Apple-Liver Rumaki 80
Artichoke Dippers 118
Avocado Bread 28
Avocado Pinwheel, Molded 112
Avocado-Egg Sandwiches 52

B
Bacon & Tomato Dip 106
Bacon-Stuffed Cherry Tomatoes 114
Baked Grapefruit Alaska 32-33
Bananas, Coconut 17
Barbecue Menu, Summer Night 100
Barbecue, Summer Night 93, 100-104
Barbecued Beef Sandwiches 88
Beans, Refried 21
Beef
   Barbecued Beef Sandwiches 88
   Beef Teriyaki 25
   Carne Asada 21
   Chafing Dish Steak Bites 119
   Fabulous Chunky Chili 107
   Shish Kabobs 102
   Steak In A Bag 96-97
Beer Batter Franks 123
Best Bran Muffins 36
Beverages 148-156
   Alcoholic
      Amber Ginger Punch 154
      Blushing Sangria 150

      Burgundy-Apple Punch 154
      Fluffy Eggnog 151
      Gala Champagne Punch 152
      Hot Spiced Rum Punch 155
      Mai Tai Punch 156
      Margaritas 150
      Sangria Blanca 150
      Special Ramos Fizz 151
      Strawberry Wine Punch 156
      Whiskey Sour Bowl 151
   Non-Alcoholic
      Company Hot Chocolate 149
      Dessert Coffee 149
      Holiday Cranberry Punch 154
      Island Fruit Punch 156
      Spiced Tea 149
      Sunshine Punch 155
Bisques
   Clam Bisque 75
   Creamed Tomato Bisque 60-61
Blintz Soufflé 38
Blue Cheese Mold 116
Blue Ribbon Carrot Cake 109
Blushing Sangria 150
Blueberry Syrup 38
Bombe, Party 68
Bonbons, Chocolate 130
Boursin Cheese Quiche 40-41
Bowl Game Buffet 74, 86-92
Bran Muffins, Best 36
Breads
   Avocado Bread 28
   Best Bran Muffins 36
   Cheese-Topped French Bread 104
   Corn Bread Casserole 107
   Crisp Crackers 73
   Crunchy Rye Bread 84
   Freezer French-Toasted Muffins 45
   High Hat Popovers 65

   Lemon Tea Bread 132
   Orange Blossom French Toast 45
   Parmesan Crescents 95
   Prune Bread 46
   Toasted Brie Wafers 128
Brie Wafers, Toasted 128
Broccoli With Olive-Nut Sauce 82
Brochettes, Chicken Liver 37
Broiled Tomatoes 96
Brunch Get-Togethers 31-48
Brunch Menus
   Family Brunch 43
   Festive Brunch 37
   Sunday Brunch 32
Buffet For A Crowd 93, 105-109
Buffet Menus (Also see Dessert
   (Buffets)
   Bowl Game Buffet 86
   Buffet For A Crowd 105
   Elegant Supper, An 75
   Holiday Open House 80
Buffet Suppers 74, 92
Burgundy-Apple Punch 154
Butter Cookie Cut-Outs 142
Butter Cookie Dough 142

C
Cake Mix Cookies 146
Cakes
   Blue Ribbon Carrot Cake 109
   Chocolate Mousse Cake 98-99
   Glazed Chocolate Cake Bars
      139-139
   Glazed Confetti Cake 91
   Lucky Lemon Cake 73
   Waldorf Torte 137
Candlelight Dinner 93-99
Candy Kiss Cookies 142
Caramel Graham Cracker Cookies 63

Card Party 49, 69-73
Carne Asada 21
Carrot Cake, Blue Ribbon 109
Carrots & Grapes, Glazed 98
Carrots, Copper Penny 90
Caviar-Stuffed Eggs 118
Celebration Picnic 49-50, 60-63
Centerpieces
      Luau Centerpiece 12-13
      Sombrero Salad 18-20
      Vegetable Basket 8-9
      Watermelon Whale 10-11
Chafing Dish Steak Bites 119
Champagne Punch, Gala 152
Champagne Shower 49-59
Cheese Bites, Chili 16
Cheese Log, Holiday 114
Cheese Soufflé, Easy 39
Cheese Soup, Velvet 69
Cheese Spread, Curried 87
Cheesecake, Chocolate Chip 140
Cheesecake Squares 131
Cheese-Topped French Bread 104
Cherry Tomatoes, Bacon-Stuffed 114
Cherry Tomatoes, Sautéed 79
Chewy Nut Bars 146
Chicken
      Chicken & Shrimp Kaanipali 27
      Chinese Chicken Salad 71
      Fruited Chicken Salad
         Sandwiches 51
      Spinach-Chicken Soufflé Roll 78
Chicken Liver Brochettes 37
Chili Cheese Bites 16
Chili, Fabulous Chunky 107
Chinese Chicken Salad 71
Chocolate Bonbons 130
Chocolate Cake Bars, Glazed 138-13
Chocolate Chip Cheesecake 140

Chocolate Chip Coffeecake 36
Chocolate Chip Treats 147
Chocolate, Company Hot 149
Chocolate Leaves 7
Chocolate Mousse Cake 98-99
Chocolate Strawberries 6
Choco-Nut Fruit Balls 147
Chutney, Peach 65
Clam Bisque 75
Clam Fondue Dip 122
Cocktail Franks, Glazed 128
Cocktail Parties 110-128
Coconut Bananas 17
Coconut Tea Sandwiches 53
Coconut, Toasted 27
Coconut-Date Macaroons 146
Coffee, Dessert 149
Coffeecake, Chocolate Chip 36
Coffeecake Fruit Squares 48
Cold Meat Salad 62
Cold Poached Salmon 56
Company Hot Chocolate 149
Condiments (Also see Relishes)
   Toasted Coconut 27
   Peach Chutney 65
Confetti Cake, Glazed 91
Cookie Exchange, Holiday 129,
   141-147
Cookie tree 129
Cookies (Also see Holiday Cookie
   Exchange)
   Caramel Graham Cracker
      Cookies 63
   Lacy Oatmeal Cookies 42
   Mexican Wedding Rings 23
   Ribbon Cookies 99
Copper Penny Carrots 90
Corn Bread Casserole 107
Cottage Cheese Pancakes 44
Crab Canapés 124
Crab Quiche, Crustless 42
Crabmeat
   Crab Canapés 124
   Crustless Crab Quiche 42
   Curried Seafood Salad 66
   Elegant Lazy-Day Soup 75
   Gazpacho Seafood Dip 116
   Seafood Tartlets 124
Crackers, Crisp 73
Cranberry Punch, Holiday 154
Cream Puff Swans 58-59
Creamed Tomato Bisque 60-61
Creamy Apricot Mold 101
Creamy Scrambled Eggs 46
Crinkles, Double-Chocolate 141
Crisp Crackers 73
Crunchy Rye Bread 84
Crustless Crab Quiche 42
Cucumber Boats With Caviar 115
Cucumber Sandwiches 53
Cucumber Sauce 55
Cucumbers In Sour Cream Sauce 77
Curried Cheese Spread 87
Curried Egg Sandwiches 52
Curried Seafood Salad 66

D
Date-Nut Bars, Holiday 143
Dessert Buffets 129
Dessert Coffee 149
Desserts (Also see Cakes, Cookies,
   Pies and Dessert Buffets)
   Baked Grapefruit Alaska 32-33
   Cream Puff Swans 58-59
   Creamy Apricot Mold 101
   English Trifle 92
   Frozen Lemon Cream 23

Fudge-Coffee Ice Cream
   Bars 104
   Lemon Snowball 85
   Party Bombe 68
   Royal Mocha Freeze 79
   Ruby Poached Pears 42
Dill Dip 117
Dill Sauce 56
Dilled Shrimp 95
Dinner Menu, A Candlelight 94
   (Also see Buffets, Barbecue,
   Fiesta and Luau)
Dinner Parties 93-110
Dips & Spreads (Also see Sandwiches)
   Bacon & Tomato Dip 106
   Blue Cheese Mold 116
   Clam Fondue Dip 122
   Curried Cheese Spread 187
   Dill Dip 117
   Fiesta Dip 106
   Gazpacho-Seafood Dip 117
   Guacamole Spread 22
   Herring Salad Appetizer 118
   Holiday Cheese Log 114
   Hummus Spread 63
   Liver Pâté Football 86
   Mock Liver Pâté 111
   Molded Avocado Pinwheel 112
   Salmon & Cream Spread 81
   Shrimp Pâté 112
   Spinach Dip 100
Double-Chocolate Crinkles 141
Dressed-Up Peanut Butter
   Sandwiches 53

E
Easy Cheese Soufflé 39
Efficient Freezing, Tips For 5
Egg Sandwiches, Curried 52
Eggnog, Fluffy 151
Eggplant Salad 62
Eggs (Also see Soufflés)
   Boursin Cheese Quiche 40-41
   Caviar-Stuffed Eggs 118
   Creamy Scrambled Eggs 46
   Crustless Crab Quiche 41
   Curried Egg Sandwiches 52
Elegant Lazy-Day Soup 75
Elegant Supper, An 74-79
English Trifle 92
Entertaining With Ease 2

F
Fabulous Chunky Chili 107
Family Brunch 31, 43-48
Festive Brunch 31, 37-42
Festive Fare 15-30
Fiesta Dip 106
Fiesta Menu, Mexican 16
Fiesta, Mexican 15-23
Fillings
   Meat Filling For Filo 125
   Triple-Cheese Filling For Filo 127
Filo Triangles 125-127
Fish and Seafood
   Chicken & Shrimp Kaanipali 27
   Cold Poached Salmon 56
   Crab Canapés 124
   Crustless Crab Quiche 41
   Curried Seafood Salad 66
   Dilled Shrimp 95
   Gazpacho-Seafood Dip 117
   Salmon & Cream Spread 81
   Salmon Mousse 55
   Seafood Tartlets 124
   Shrimp Pâté 112
Flash freeze 5
Flowers, frosted 68

Fluffy Eggnog 151
Fluffy Fruit Dressing 139
Fondue Dip, Clam 122
Franks
   Beer Batter Franks 123
   Glazed Cocktail Franks 128
Freeze Now—Enjoy Later 4-5
Freezer French-Toasted Muffins 45
French Toast, Orange Blossom 45
French-Style Potatoes 97
French-Toasted Muffins, Freezer 45
Frosted Flowers 68
Frosted Fruit Salad 72
Frozen Lemon Cream 23
Fruit Balls, Choco-Nut 147
Fruit Kabobs 63
Fruit Mold, Frozen 108
Fruit Mold, Lemon 77
Fruit Salad, Frosted 72
Fruit Salad, Marinated 39
Fruit Soup, Raspberry-Wine 64
Fruit Squares, Coffeecake 48
Fruit Tartlets, Glazed 133
Fruited Chicken Salad Sandwiches 51
Fudge Nut Sauce 57
Fudge-Coffee Ice Cream Bars 104

G
Gala Champagne Punch 152
Gala Garnishes 6-14
Garnishes
   Chocolate Leaves 7
   Chocolate Strawberries 6
   Fluted Vegetables 9
   Frosted Flowers 68
   Radish Fans, Roses & Tulips 8-9
   Sugar & Spice Grapes 6
   Tomato Rose 14
   Turnip Daisies 9
   Vegetable Basket 8-9
Gazpacho-Seafood Dip 117
Ginger Punch, Amber 154
Glazed Carrots & Grapes 98
Glazed Chocolate Cake Bars 138-139
Glazed Cocktail Franks 128
Glazed Confetti Cake 91
Glazed Fruit Tartlets 133
Glazed Ham Steak 44
Graham Cracker Cookies, Caramel 63
Grapefruit Alaska, Baked 32-33
Grapes, Sugar & Spice 6
Green Beans With Cashews 29
Guacamole Spread 22

H
Ham
   Glazed Ham Steak 44
   Jeweled Buffet Ham 81
Herring Salad Appetizer 118
High Hat Popovers 65
Holiday Cheese Log 114
Holiday Cookie Exchange 129,
   141-147
Holiday Cranberry Punch 154
Holiday Date-Nut Bars 143
Holiday Open House 74, 80-85
Hors d'Oeuvres (Also see Dips &
   Spreads and Sandwiches)
   Cold Hors d'Oeuvres 111-118
   Dilled Shrimp 95
   Hot Hors d'Oeuvres 119-128
   Apple-Liver Rumaki 80
   Chicken Liver Brochettes 37
   Chili Cheese Bites 16
   Mexican Meatballs 17
   Parmesan Crescents 95
   Sausage Puffs 33
   Spinach Pom Poms 87

Won Ton Bows With Sweet &
   Sour Sauce 24-25
Hot Chocolate, Company 149
Hot Spiced Rum Punch 155
How Much For How Many 157
Hummus Spread 63

I
Ice Ring 152
Island Fruit Punch 156
Island Luau 15, 24-30
Island Spareribs 26

J
Jeweled Buffet Ham 81

K
Kabobs, Fruit 63
Kona Crunch Pie 30

L
Lacy Oatmeal Cookies 42
Lamb
   Shish Kabobs 102
Lazy-Day Soup, Elegant 75
Leaves, Chocolate 7
Lemon Cake, Lucky 73
Lemon Cream, Frozen 23
Lemon Fruit Mold 77
Lemon Snowball 85
Lemon Tea Bread 132
Lemon-Almond Tartlets 136
Lime Angel Pie 29
Litchi Nuts, Stuffed 117
Liver
   Apple-Liver Rumaki 80
   Chicken Liver Brochettes 37
   Liver Pâté Football 86
   Mock Liver Pâté 111
Loving Kisses 144
Luau Centerpiece 12-13
Luau Menu, Island 24
Lucky Lemon Cake 73
Luncheon Menus
   Card Party 69
   Celebration Picnic 60
   Champagne Shower 51
   Special Occasion, A 64
Luncheons 49-73

M
Macaroons, Coconut-Date 146
Mai Tai Mold 26
Mai Tai Punch 156
Make Ahead Makes It Easy 2
Margaritas 150
Marinated Fruit Salad 39
Marinated Stuffed Mushrooms 115
Marinated Vegetable Salad 108
Marainated Zucchini Salad 57
Meat Filling for Filo 125
Meat Salad, Cold 62
Meatballs, Mexican 17
Mediterranean Pilaf 102
Menu Substitutions 5
Menus
   Afternoon Tea 130
   Bowl Game Buffet 86
   Buffet For A Crowd 105
   Candlelight Dinner, A 94
   Card Party 69
   Celebration Picnic 60
   Champagne Shower 51
   Elegant Supper, An 75
   Family Brunch 43
   Festive Brunch 37

159

Index

Holiday Cookie Exchange 141
Holiday Open House 80
Island Luau 24
Mexican Fiesta 16
Shaping The Menu To Fit The
Party 5
Special Occasion, A 64
Substitutions 5
Summer Night Barbecue 100
Sunday Brunch 32
Sweet Table Reception 136
Mexican Fiesta 15-23
Mexican Meatballs 17
Mexican Wedding Rings 23
Middle Eastern Relish 61
Mocha Freeze, Royal 79
Molded Avocado Pinwheel 112-113
Mousse Cake, Chocolate 98-99
Mousse, Mustard 83
Mousse, Salmon 55
Muffins, Best Bran 36
Muffins, Freezer French-Toasted 45
Mushrooms, Pâté-Stuffed 125
Mushrooms, Marinated Stuffed 115
Mustard Mousse 83
Mustard Sauce, Spicy 123

N
Nature's Tuna Salad 62
Niçoise, Salade 70-71
Noodle Pudding Soufflé 82
Nut Bars, Chewy 146

O
Oatmeal Cookies, Lacy 42
Open-Face Sandwiches 50
Open House, Holiday 74, 80-85
Open House Menu, Holiday 80
Orange Blossom French Toast 45
Orange Syrup 48
Overnight Buffet Salad 90

P
Pancakes
Apple Puffed Pancake 34
Cottage Cheese Pancakes 44
Potato Pancakes 43
Puffed Pancake With
Strawberries 34
Parmesan Crescents 95
Party Bombe 68
Pâtés
Liver Pâté Football 86
Mock Liver Pâté 111
Shrimp Pâté 112
Pâté-Stuffed Mushrooms 125
Peach Chutney 65
Peanut Butter Jewels 144
Peanut Butter Sandwiches,
Dressed-Up 53
Pears, Ruby Poached 40
Picnic, Celebration 49-50, 60-63
Picnic Menu, Celebration 60
Pies
Kona Crunch Pie 30
Lime Angel Pie 29
Pineapple-Beet Mold 91
Pita Bread Sandwiches 50
Popovers, High Hat 65
Pork
Island Spareribs 26
Sausage Puffs 33
Potato Pancakes 43
Potaotes, French-Style 97
Prune Bread 46
Puffed Pancake With Strawberries 34
Punch, see Beverages

Q
Quiche, Boursin Cheese 40-41
Quiche, Crustless Crab 42

R
Ramos Fizz, Special 151
Rarebit Savories 120
Raspberry-Wine Fruit Soup 64
Refried Beans 21
Relishes (Also see Condiments)
Middle Eastern Relish 61
Mustard Mousse 83
Salsa 22
Ribbon Cookies 99
Rice
Mediterranean Pilaf 102
Royal Mocha Freeze 79
Ruby Poached Pears 40
Rum Punch, Hot Spiced 155
Rye Bread, Crunchy 84

S
Salade Niçoise 70-71
Salads
Chinese Chicken Salad 71
Cold Meat Salad 62
Creamy Apricot Mold 101
Cucumbers In Sour Cream 77
Curried Seafood Salad 5
Eggplant Salad 62
Frosted Fruit Salad 72
Frozen Fruit Mold 108
Guacamole Spread 22
Herring Salad Appetizer 118
Lemon Fruit Mold 77
Mai Tai Mold 26
Marinated Fruit Salad 39
Marinated Vegetable Salad 108
Marinated Zucchini Salad 57
Nature's Tuna Salad 62
Overnight Buffet Salad 90
Pineapple-Beet Mold 91
Ready Slaw 101
Salade Niçoise 70-71
Sombrero Salad 20
Sunshine Salad 84
Tropical Salad Bowl 28
Salmon & Cream Spread 81
Salmon, Cold Poached 56
Salmon Mousse 55
Salsa 22
Sandwiches
Avocado-Egg Sandwiches 52
Barbecued Beef Sandwiches 88
Coconut Tea Sandwiches 53
Cucumber Sandwiches 53
Curried Egg Sandwiches 52
Dressed-Up Peanut Butter
Sandwiches 53
Fruited Chicken Salad
Sandwiches 51
Open-Face Sandwiches 50
Pita Bread Sandwiches 50
Sangria Blanca 150
Sangria, Blushing 150
Sauces
Blueberry Syrup 38
Cucumber Sauce 55
Dill Sauce 56
Fluffy Fruit Dressing 139
Fudge Nut Sauce 57
Orange Syrup 48
Spicy Mustard Sauce 123
Sausage Puffs 33
Sautéed Cherry Tomatoes 79
Scrambled Eggs, Creamy 46
Seafood, see Fish and Seafood

Seafood Tartlets 124
Serving Your Guests 2
Sesame Seed Turnovers 120
Shaping The Menu To Fit The Party 5
Shish Kabobs 102
Shower Menu, Champagne 51
Shrimp
Chicken & Shrimp Kaanipali 27
Curried Seafood Salad 66
Dilled Shrimp 95
Gazpacho Seafood Dip 116
Seafood Tartlets 124
Shrimp Pâté 112
Sombrero Salad 20
Soufflés
Blintz Soufflé 38
Easy Cheese Soufflé 39
Noodle Pudding Soufflé 82
Spinach Soufflé Triangles 126-127
Spinach-Chicken Soufflé Roll 78
Soups
Clam Bisque 75
Creamed Tomato Bisque 60-61
Elegant Lazy-Day Soup 75
Raspberry-Wine Fruit Soup 64
Velvet Cheese Soup 69
Zucchini Soup 94
Spareribs, Island 26
Special Occasion, A 64-68
Special Ramos Fizz 151
Spiced Tea 149
Spicy Mustard Sauce 123
Spinach Dip 100
Spinach Pom Poms 87
Spinach Soufflé Triangles 126-127
Spinach-Chicken Soufflé Roll 78
Spreads, see Dips & Spreads and
Sandwiches
Steak Bites, Chafing Dish 119
Steak In A Bag 96-97
Strawberries, Chocolate 6
Strawberry Wine Punch 156
Stuffed Litchi Nuts 117
Sugar & Spice Grapes 6
Summer Night Barbecue 93, 100-104
Sunday Brunch 31-36
Sunshine Punch 155
Sunshine Salad 84
Swans, Cream Puff 58-59
Sweet Table Reception 129, 136-140
Syrup, Blueberry 38
Syrup, Orange 48

T
Tables
Freeze Now-Enjoy Later 13
How Much For How Many 157
Taco Tartlets 122
Tartlets
Glazed Fruit Tartlets 133
Lemon-Almond Tartlets 136
Seafood Tartlets 124
Taco Tartlets 122
Tea Menu, Afternoon 130
Tea Sandwiches, Coconut 53
Tea, Spiced 149
Teriyaki Beef 25
Tips For Efficient Freezing 5
Toasted Brie Wafers 128
Toasted Coconut 27
Tomato Bisque, Creamed 60-61
Tomato Rose 14
Tomatoes, Bacon-Stuffed Cherry 114
Tomatoes, Broiled 96
Torte, Waldorf 137
Triangles, Filo 125-127
Trifle, English 92

Triple-Cheese Filling For Filo 127
Tropical Salad Bowl 28
Tuna Salad, Nature's 62
Turnovers, Sesame Seed 120

V
Vegetable Basket 8-9
Vegetable Salad, Marinated 108
Vegetables (Also see Salads)
Aritchoke Dippers 118
Broccoli With Olive-Nut Sauce 82
Broiled Tomatoes 96
Copper Penny Carrots 90
Cucumbers In Sour Cream Sauce
French-Style Potatoes 97
Glazed Carrots & Grapes 98
Green Beans With Cashews 29
Sautéed Cherry Tomatoes 79
Spinach Dip 100
Spinach Pom Poms 87
Spinach Soufflé Triangles 128
Spinach-Chicken Soufflé Roll 78
Vegetable Basket 8-9
Velvet Cheese Soup 69

W
Wafers, Toasted Brie 128
Waldorf Torte 137
Watermelon Whale 10-11
Wedding Rings 23
Whiskey Sour Bowl 151
Won Ton Bows With Sweet & Sour
Sauce 24-25

Z
Zucchini Salad, Marinated 57
Zucchini Soup 94

9.431204781628